D0181500

→ INTRODUCING

LINGUISTICS

R.L. TRASK & BILL MAYBLIN

ICON

This edition published in
the UK and the USA
in 2009 by Icon Books Ltd,
Omnibus Business Centre,
39–41 North Road, London N7 9DP
email: info@iconbooks.com
www.introducingbooks.com

Sold in the UK, Europe and Asia
by Faber & Faber Ltd,
Bloomsbury House,
74–77 Great Russell Street,
London WC1B 3DA or their agents

Distributed in South Africa
by Jonathan Ball,
Office B4, The District,
41 Sir Lowry Road,
Woodstock 7925

Distributed in Australia and
New Zealand
by Allen & Unwin Pty Ltd,
PO Box 8500, 83 Alexander Street,
Crows Nest, NSW 2065

Distributed in the USA
by Publishers Group West,
1700 Fourth Street,
Berkeley, CA 94710

Distributed in Canada
by Publishers Group Canada,
76 Stafford Street, Unit 300
Toronto, Ontario M6J 2S1

Previously published in the UK and
Australia in 2000

ISBN: 978-184831-088-9

Text and illustrations copyright © 2012 Icon Books Ltd

The author and artist have asserted their moral rights.

Originating editor: Richard Appignanesi

Printed and bound in Great Britain by Clays Ltd, Elcograf S.p.A.

A Brief History of Linguistics

Human beings have probably been speaking for as long as we have existed, but it was only around 3,000 years ago that anybody began to be curious about language and to start examining it. This happened independently in two places.

GRAMMATICAL ANALYSIS DEVELOPED VERY EARLY IN ANCIENT INDIA.

A DESCRIPTION OF GRAMMAR ALSO APPEARED AMONG ANCIENT GREEKS.

We might begin with an example from the Indian tradition.

An Indian Linguist

Pāṇini's life (*circa* 5th century BC) is unknown, but his work, the *Aṣṭādhayayī*, is a culmination of earlier studies in phonology and grammar.

Pāṇini's approach to grammar requires that the pieces of words should first be glued together in order. Rules should then be applied to convert these sequences into the correct surface forms. Pāṇini worked on Sanskrit, but we can illustrate his method very well with English. Consider the verb

penetrate

and its related adjective

impenetrable

meaning "not able to be penetrated". This consists of the negative prefix

in – (as in insane),

the stem **penetrate**

and the suffix – **ble**

So, to start with, we have

in-penetrate-ble

Now we need some rules, which we will apply to pronunciation, not necessarily to spelling.

First, if a verb-stem ends in *-ate* immediately followed by another consonant (like *b*), drop the *t* of the verb-stem.

Second, if we now have a long **A** sound followed by the suffix *-ble*, change this long **A** to the weak vowel found in the last syllable of *circus* and *carrot*.

Third, if an *n* is immediately followed by a consonant pronounced with the lips, like *b*, change the *n* to *m*.

These rules produce the required result:

impenetrable

I'LL BE DOING SOMETHING LIKE THIS ... BUT MUCH, MUCH LATER!

Pāṇini's formal style of phonological analysis looks ahead 2,000 years to Noam Chomsky's approach in the 1960s – and, in fact, Chomsky has acknowledged his tribute to the Indian grammarian.

The Greek Origins of Linguistics

Even though the Indian tradition was much the more sophisticated of the two, it was the Greeks who founded the European tradition.

The great Greek scholar Aristotle (384–322 BC) took the first step.

The Greek verb **leípō** "leave", like any Greek verb, has more than 300 distinct forms.

*I DIVIDED THE SENTENCE INTO TWO PARTS CALLED THE **SUBJECT** AND THE **PREDICATE**.*

leípein to leave

leípōn leaving

leípsein to be going to leave

leípsōn going to leave

lipein having left

leípō I leave

leípeis you (singular) leave

leípei he/she leaves

leípomen we leave

leípete you (plural) leave

leípousi they leave

leípō (that) I may leave

leipoimi may I leave

leípsō I will leave

leípsoimi may I leave (future)

élipon I left

lípō (that) I might leave

lípoimi might I have left

léloipa I have left

eleloípē I had left

leípomai I remain

SUBJECT:
The King of Persia

PREDICATE:
took a vast army into Greece.

Aristotle went no further, but this division is still recognized today, as a fundamental part of the analysis of sentences.

leípomai I will remain

elipómēn I remained

léleimmai I have remained

leiphthḗsomai I will be left

elíphthen I was left

Grammar or Parts of Speech

The Greek work culminated in the writings of Apollonius Dyscolus (110–175 AD) and Dionysius Thrax (second to first centuries BC). It was Thrax who produced the first complete grammar of Greek, only parts of which survive today. Ancient Greek was a language in which most words could take lots and lots of different endings for grammatical purposes.

By looking at the behaviour of Greek words, and especially at these endings, Thrax concluded that Greek words fell into just eight classes, which we call the *parts of speech*.

Thrax's description of Greek would become the basis of all grammatical description in Europe until well into the 20th century, even though his eight classes were later modified.

Latin Grammar

After the Roman conquest of Greece in the mid-2nd century BC, Roman scholars learned of the Greek work, and they began to apply the same analysis to their own language, Latin.

THIS COPYING DIDN'T TURN OUT TOO BADLY, BECAUSE LATIN WAS RATHER SIMILAR TO GREEK IN ITS STRUCTURE.

amicus bonus a good friend

amici boni of a good friend

amico bono to a good friend

amicum bonum a good friend (object)

amico bono (by/with/from) a good friend

amici boni good friends

amicorum bonorum of good friends

amicis bonis to good friends

amicos bonos good friends (object)

amicis bonis (by/with/from) good friends

The Graeco-Latin tradition was ultimately synthesized in the work of the most influential Roman grammarian, Priscian, who wrote in the 6th century AD. Priscian's description of Latin is still what we find in most school textbooks of Latin today.

When Europeans finally began to be interested in writing descriptions of their own languages in the 14th and 15th centuries, they mostly tried to impose Priscian's account of Latin onto their own languages.

THIS WAS SOMEWHAT UNFORTUNATE, SINCE SPANISH, FRENCH, GERMAN AND ITALIAN ARE NOT ALWAYS VERY SIMILAR TO LATIN.

WHILE ENGLISH IS VERY DIFFERENT INDEED.

Traditional Grammar

Nevertheless, this *traditional Graeco-Roman grammar* has continued to be taught in European schools down to the present day.

Except that, in the English-speaking countries, the teaching of English grammar was largely discontinued in the 1960s...

IN THE BELIEF THAT GRAMMAR WAS TOO BORING TO ENGAGE THE ATTENTION OF SCHOOL PUPILS.

The conjunctive pronoun 'who' makes an adverbial clause whenever it is substituted for a subordinative conjunction.

The Port-Royal Grammar

The 17th-century French scholars, known as the Port-Royal Circle, put together a remarkably original "universal" grammar of French, one which largely broke free from the Priscianic tradition. Here is a typical example of their analyses.

The invisible God created the visible world.

This sentence is analysed as...

God, who is invisible, created the world, which is visible

... which in turn is decomposed into the three propositions...

God is invisible

God created the world

The world is visible

THIS ANALYSIS IS STRIKINGLY SIMILAR TO MY EARLIEST 1950s VERSION OF TRANSFORMATIONAL GRAMMAR.

N. Chomsky

The German polymath Wilhelm von Humboldt (1767–1835), brother of the famous explorer Alexander von Humboldt, likewise tried to develop a universalist and philosophical approach to the study of languages.

The central fact of language is that speakers can make infinite use of the finite resources provided by their language. Though the capacity for language is universal, the individuality of each language is a property of the people who speak it. Every language has its *innere Sprachform*, or internal structure, which determines its outer form and which is the reflection of its speakers' minds. The language and the thought of a people are thus inseparable.

A PEOPLE'S SPEECH IS THEIR SPIRIT,

AND THEIR SPIRIT IS THEIR SPEECH.

Although Humboldt's work excited a good deal of attention, it too failed to establish a continuing tradition.

Historical Linguistics

Toward the close of the 18th century, European linguists began to realize that certain languages exhibited such striking systematic resemblances that they must be derived from a single common ancestor, from which they had diverged by a long series of changes. Scholars like Franz Bopp (1791–1867), Rasmus Rask (1787–1832) and Jakob Grimm (1785–1863) were able to show that almost all of the languages of Europe and many languages of Asia were all related in this way.

*THIS FAMILY OF LANGUAGES, CALLED THE **INDO-EUROPEAN** FAMILY, IS ULTIMATELY DESCENDED FROM A REMOTE ANCESTOR ...*

As a result of these astonishing discoveries, the study of language change and of the prehistories of languages, called *historical linguistics*, came to be by far the most important way of studying languages, and other approaches were temporarily submerged.

*WHICH WE CALL **PROTO-INDO-EUROPEAN.***

Jakob Grimm

Rasmus Rask

Franz Bopp

Here's an example of the kind of systematic correspondence that attracted early attention. Note the initial consonants.

English	Latin	Greek
fish	piscis	(ikhthys)
father	pater	pater
foot	ped-	pod-
for	pro	para
six	sex	hexa
seven	septem	hepta
sweet	suavis	hedys
salt	sal	hal
new	novus	neos
night	noct-	nykt-
nine	novem	(en)nea

The Origins of General Linguistics

Only toward the end of the 19th century did the non-historical study of language structure begin to reassert itself. Pioneers like the German Georg von der Gabelentz (1840–93) and the Poles Jan Baudouin de Courtenay (1845–1929) and Mikołai Kruszewski (1851–87) published important observations about word structure and sound structure in languages.

This kind of work we now call *general linguistics*: the study of how languages are put together and how they work.

Ferdinand de Saussure

But the single most influential figure in the development of general linguistics was, at this time, working in some obscurity in the Swiss city of Geneva. Ferdinand de Saussure (1857–1913) had been trained as a historical linguist, and in fact he had made important contributions to the understanding of Proto-Indo-European. Saussure applied the technique of internal reconstruction to Proto-Indo-European (PIE) to explain certain irregularities in the forms of some roots. Most PIE roots have the form *CeC-*, where *C* means "any consonant". For instance ...

bʰel-	'shine'
bʰer-	'carry'
gel-	'form into a ball'
kwel-	'revolve'
meg-	'great'
mel-	'soft'
nebʰ-	'cloud'
ped-	'foot'
reg-	'go straight'
sed-	'sit'

ag-	'lead'
ak-	'sharp'
dʰe:-	'put, set'
do:-	'give'
ed-	'eat'
es-	'be'
ma:-	'good'
od-	'smell'
se:-	'sow'

BUT SOME ARE DIFFERENT. THE VOWEL IS A OR O INSTEAD OF E. THE FIRST OR THE LAST CONSONANT IS MISSING. AND, WHEN THE LAST CONSONANT IS MISSING, THE VOWEL IS LONG (MARKED BY A COLON):

Saussure proposed that these irregular roots had earlier been perfectly regular, but that they had happened to contain certain consonants which had disappeared. We now call these consonants *laryngeals*.

15

Saussure's Lectures on General Linguistics

Most people reduce language to a list of terms corresponding to a list of things. For instance, in Latin ...

EQUUS

ARBOR

A LINGUISTIC SIGN IS NOT A LINK BETWEEN A THING AND A NAME, BUT BETWEEN A CONCEPT AND A SOUND-PATTERN. THE SOUND PATTERN IS NOT ACTUALLY A SOUND, FOR A SOUND IS SOMETHING PHYSICAL. A SOUND PATTERN IS THE HEARER'S PSYCHOLOGICAL IMPRESSION OF A SOUND.

In the early years of the 20th century, Saussure began lecturing on general linguistics at the University of Geneva. Saussure's highly original ideas captured the imagination of his students. Saussure died without ever publishing his ideas.

BUT WE POOLED AND EDITED OUR LECTURE NOTES AND PUBLISHED, IN 1916, A VOLUME WITH SAUSSURE'S NAME ON IT ...

... the now-celebrated *Cours*.

Saussure's Structuralism

Before Saussure, most linguists had taken an *atomistic* approach to language structure. That is, they perceived a language as primarily a collection of objects, such as speech sounds, words and grammatical endings.

*I ARGUED INSTEAD THAT A LANGUAGE WAS BEST REGARDED AS A **STRUCTURED SYSTEM** OF ELEMENTS, IN WHICH THE PLACE OF EACH ELEMENT IS DEFINED CHIEFLY BY HOW IT **RELATES** TO OTHER ELEMENTS.*

ME

MY

This novel approach quickly came to be called *structuralism,* and, since Saussure's work, virtually all important work on languages has been structuralist in this sense.

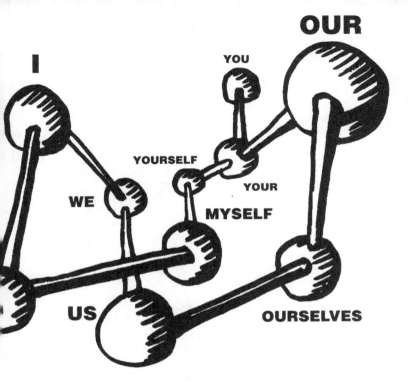

An Example from English

Here is an example of structuralist analysis. Among the speech sounds found in English are two which we represent as [**d**] and as [**ð**].

The sound [**d**] occurs at the beginning of the word *den*,

while the sound [**ð**] occurs at the beginning of the word *then*.

Since these words are otherwise identical in pronunciation, and since they have different meanings, we may therefore conclude that these two sounds "count" as different in English. That is, they behave as two different structural units for the purpose of building English words. We therefore say that [**d**] and [**ð**] belong, in English, to two different structural units, or *phonemes*, which we represent as /**d**/ and /**ð**/, so that *den* and *then* are represented phonemically as /den/ and /ðen/.

An Example from Spanish

de[ð]o

In contrast, the sounds [**d**] and [**ð**] exist also in Spanish, but their behaviour is different there. In Spanish, [**ð**] can occur only in certain positions, notably between vowels, as in [deðo] "finger", while [**d**] can never occur in these positions.

Note, for example, [dama] "lady", with [**d**], but [la ðama] "the lady", with [**ð**] between vowels.

In Spanish, therefore, the two sounds do not "count" as different, and we assign them both to a single phoneme [d]. The correctness of this analysis is recognized by the Spanish spelling system, which writes *dedo*, "finger", *dama*, "lady" and *la dama*, "the lady".

[d]ama

but

la [ð]ama

Both English and Spanish possess the speech sounds [**d**] and [**ð**], then, but the structural relation between the two is different in the two languages – and, in a structuralist approach, it is the *structural relation* that matters, not the objective phonetic facts.

Today almost all work in linguistics is structuralist in Saussure's general linguistic sense. From the rules of pronunciation to the structure of conversations, linguists see a language as an orderly system, or better as a system of systems, with all linguistic phenomena forming part of these systems.

Synchronic and Diachronic Structures

A further aspect of Saussure's work is an emphasis upon two very different approaches to the study of language: a *synchronic* approach, in which we focus on the structure of a language at a particular moment in time (not necessarily the present), and a *diachronic* approach, in which we look at the development of a language over time.

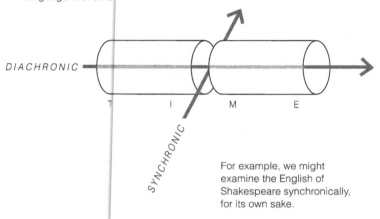

DIACHRONIC

SYNCHRONIC

T I M E

For example, we might examine the English of Shakespeare synchronically, for its own sake.

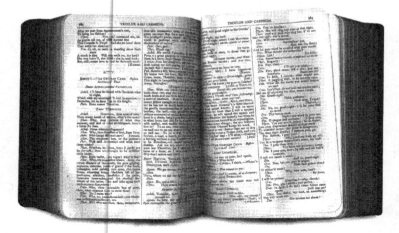

Or we might examine it diachronically, as a stage in the development of medieval English into modern English.

The Prague Circle

After the First World War, a number of East European linguists, many of them Russians fleeing the Communist revolution in Russia (1917), congregated in the Czech city of Prague. Eventually known as the Prague Circle, this group developed structuralist ideas in a number of directions during the next two decades. Particularly prominent were the Russians Nikolai Trubetzkoy (1890–1938) and Roman Jakobson (1896–1982). Trubetzkoy's *Principles of Phonology*, published in 1939, was perhaps the Circle's most influential publication (phonology is the study of sound systems in languages). But the Nazi annexation of Czechoslovakia in 1938 caused the dispersal of the group: Trubetzkoy died, while Jakobson fled west, eventually arriving in the USA.

Trubetzkoy's Phonology

Here is an example of Trubetzkoy's analysis of phonology from his book.

> The specific character of a phonological opposition consists in the latter's being *a distinctive opposition of sound* ....The concept of distinctiveness presupposes the concept of opposition. One thing can be distinguished only from another thing: it can be distinguished only insofar as it is contrasted with or opposed to something else.

For example, the word *caught* is pronounced about the same in American and Canadian accents. However, in most American accents, *caught* is pronounced differently from *cot*, while in Canadian accents *caught* and *cot* are pronounced identically.

SO, AMERICAN ACCENTS MAKE A DISTINCTION BETWEEN TWO OPPOSING VOWELS.

WHILE CANADIAN ACCENTS DO NOT.

IT IS THE DISTINCTION (OR ITS ABSENCE) WHICH IS IMPORTANT, NOT THE PRONUNCIATIONS THEMSELVES.

Jakobson's Work on Linguistics

Here is an example of Jakobson's linguistic analysis from his famous article on child language acquisition and the degree of universality of speech sounds.

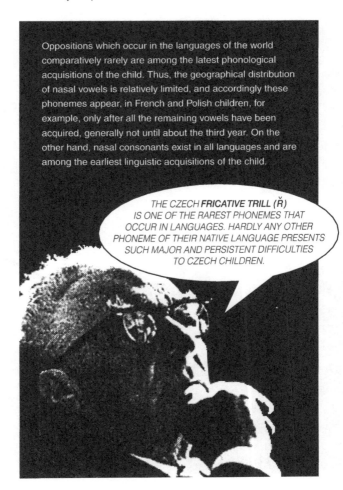

Oppositions which occur in the languages of the world comparatively rarely are among the latest phonological acquisitions of the child. Thus, the geographical distribution of nasal vowels is relatively limited, and accordingly these phonemes appear, in French and Polish children, for example, only after all the remaining vowels have been acquired, generally not until about the third year. On the other hand, nasal consonants exist in all languages and are among the earliest linguistic acquisitions of the child.

*THE CZECH **FRICATIVE TRILL (Ř)** IS ONE OF THE RAREST PHONEMES THAT OCCUR IN LANGUAGES. HARDLY ANY OTHER PHONEME OF THEIR NATIVE LANGUAGE PRESENTS SUCH MAJOR AND PERSISTENT DIFFICULTIES TO CZECH CHILDREN.*

Jakobson and Semiotics

Jakobson is a key figure bridging the development of *semiotics* from linguistics. His itinerary of exile from Russia to America links together these traditions. Linguistics provided the model of analysing language as a structured system that "produces meanings". Semiotics attempts to extend this approach to other *non-linguistic* systems, that is, to every aspect of social experience that can be analysed as structured systems of *signs*. These might include traffic systems, symphonies or architecture, and, at its most ambitious, in bio-semiotics, the evolutionary environment of organisms.

Jakobson arrives in America, 1941, and meets another tradition of semiotics ...

C. S. Peirce (1839–1914) begins working on his "semiotic" theory of signs in 1869 ...

Charles Morris (1901–79), influenced by structuralist linguist Leonard Bloomfield (1887–1949), contributes a behaviourist foundation to semiotics ...

Morris's student, Hungarian-born Thomas Sebeok (b.1920), extends semiotics to biology ...

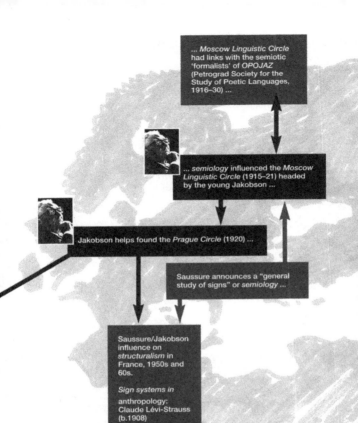

... *Moscow Linguistic Circle* had links with the semiotic 'formalists' of *OPOJAZ* (Petrograd Society for the Study of Poetic Languages, 1916–30) ...

... *semiology* influenced the *Moscow Linguistic Circle* (1915–21) headed by the young Jakobson ...

Jakobson helps found the *Prague Circle* (1920) ...

Saussure announces a "general study of signs" or *semiology* ...

Saussure/Jakobson influence on *structuralism* in France, 1950s and 60s.

Sign systems in

anthropology:
Claude Lévi-Strauss (b.1908)

psychology:
Jacques Lacan (1901–81)

history:
Michel Foucault (1926–84)

Post-structuralism

Roland Barthes (1915–80)

Jacques Derrida (b.1930)

Julia Kristeva (b.1941)

Linguistics can be, and is, performed without reference to semiotics. But semiotics is unimaginable without linguistics.

The Origins of American Linguistics

Around the time that Saussure was giving his lectures, the German-American anthropologist Franz Boas (1858–1942) was pursuing the study of the dying cultures of native Americans. Boas realized early that good investigation of these cultures required knowledge of their languages. He attacked the common prejudice that race, culture and language are part and parcel. The example he gave was of the Athapaskan linguistic families.

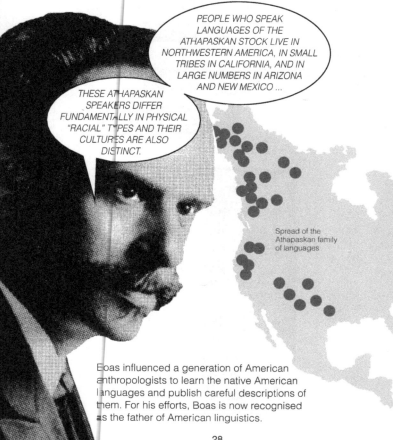

PEOPLE WHO SPEAK LANGUAGES OF THE ATHAPASKAN STOCK LIVE IN NORTHWESTERN AMERICA, IN SMALL TRIBES IN CALIFORNIA, AND IN LARGE NUMBERS IN ARIZONA AND NEW MEXICO ...

THESE ATHAPASKAN SPEAKERS DIFFER FUNDAMENTALLY IN PHYSICAL "RACIAL" TYPES AND THEIR CULTURES ARE ALSO DISTINCT.

Spread of the Athapaskan family of languages

Boas influenced a generation of American anthropologists to learn the native American languages and publish careful descriptions of them. For his efforts, Boas is now recognised as the father of American linguistics.

28

Sapir's General Linguistics

Boas's most famous student was another German-American, Edward Sapir (1884–1939). Sapir came to linguistics with a strong background in music, art and literature, and his approach to language was accordingly broad and humane in outlook. Sapir was deeply interested in uncovering possible relations between language and culture.

"WHOM DID YOU SEE?" IS THE CORRECT FORM. BUT THE NATURAL ONE IS "WHO DID YOU SEE?"

WE MUST LOOK TO THE UNCONTROLLED SPEECH OF THE FOLK FOR ADVANCE INFORMATION ON GENERAL LINGUISTIC TRENDS.

"WHOM" WILL ONE DAY BECOME AS ARCHAIC AS THE ELIZABETHAN "HIS" FOR "ITS".

Sapir's classic 1921 book *Language*, the first English-language textbook of general linguistics, established a tradition of humane language studies which is still pursued today.

The Sapir-Whorf Hypothesis

Sapir's best-known student, a former fire-insurance inspector named Benjamin Lee Whorf (1897–1941), pursued his teacher's interests and produced a number of studies of native American and Canadian languages. Pointing to striking differences in the way that different languages carve up the world, Whorf produced a cultural argument.

THE STRUCTURE OF OUR LANGUAGE MUST, TO SOME EXTENT, DETERMINE THE WAY WE PERCEIVE THE WORLD.

This idea, variously called the *Sapir-Whorf hypothesis* or the *linguistic relativity hypothesis*, has fascinated linguists, anthropologists and psychologists ever since, though its degree of validity, if any, has been much debated.

Example of the Sapir-Whorf Hypothesis

For example, the Navaho language of Arizona is rich in words for talking about lines of various shapes, colours and configurations. Among the hundred or so words available for this purpose are *adziisgai*, 'a group of parallel white lines running off into the distance', *ahééhesgai*, 'more than two white lines forming concentric circles' and *alhch'inidzigai*, 'two white lines coming together at a point'.

This large vocabulary allows Navaho speakers to speak easily about all kinds of geometrical arrangements which would require lengthy descriptions in English.

WE PERCEIVE IT IN THE GEOMETRICAL TERMS PROVIDED SO NATURALLY BY OUR LANGUAGE.

BUT THE IMPORTANT SUGGESTION IS THAT NAVAHO SPEAKERS ACTUALLY PERCEIVE THE WORLD DIFFERENTLY FROM ENGLISH SPEAKERS.

A Pioneer of American Structuralism

Another linguist was turning American linguistics somewhat away from its anthropological and cultural connections, and toward a more tightly focused concentration on language structure in its own right. Though trained as a specialist in the Germanic languages of Europe, Leonard Bloomfield (1887–1949) first made his name by demonstrating that the techniques of historical linguistics, already applied so successfully to European and Asian languages ...

... COULD BE APPLIED WITH EQUAL SUCCESS TO NATIVE AMERICAN LANGUAGES.

Cree	Menomini	Ojibwa	Proto-Algonquian	English
atim	anɛɛm	anim	*aθemwa	dog
niitim	nenem	niinim :	*niiθemwa	my sister-in-law
kaateew	kianɛɛw	kaanaat	*kyaaθeewa	he hides him
atameek	anaameɛk	(doesn't exist)	*aθameekwa	dead fish

Bloomfield produced a masterly study of the Algonquian family of languages of North America, for which he was able to reconstruct an unrecorded *Proto-Algonquian* ancestor.

But Bloomfield became best known for his 1933 textbook, also called *Language*, in which he presented a carefully articulated approach to the structuralist analysis of languages, far more explicit and detailed than Saussure's *Cours* had been. This is exemplified by his approach to the grammatical nature of gender systems.

> The gender system of animate and inanimate in an Algonquian language, for instance, includes among the animates some things which we do not regard as living: *stone, pipe, raspberry* (but not *strawberry*), *knee* (but not *elbow*).

Ethnologic observations show that the speakers do not (except in the grammatical forms of their language) make any differential distinctions.

WE DON'T SAY "A RASPBERRY HAS LIFE; A STRAWBERRY HAS NOT", NOR DO WE MAKE A CORRESPONDING DIFFERENCE IN ANY OTHER WAY, FOR INSTANCE, IN OUR FOOD HABITS OR RELIGIOUS CEREMONY.

Post-Bloomfieldian Structruralists

The next generation of American linguists took their inspiration mainly from Bloomfield. Impatient with what they saw as the armchair theorizing of European linguists, these *post-Bloomfieldians* were eager to place linguistics upon a firmly empirical and scientific footing. The brand of linguistics they developed, known as American structuralism, therefore focused strongly on empirical data collected from hands-on fieldwork on real languages, mostly little-known languages with no written tradition.

This approach greatly expanded our understanding of what human languages could be like, but it also led its followers to be nervous about attempting generalizations, and even a little hostile to linguistic theorizing.

The Formalism of Zellig Harris

In great contrast to their European colleagues, the American structuralists took no interest in the meanings or functions of words and utterances, preferring to concentrate on linguistic forms alone. This taste was taken to something of an extreme by one unusual American linguist, Zellig Harris (1909–92) who grew ever more interested in linguistic analysis of a highly formal kind, even of an algebraic kind.

Harris was largely interested in relating sentences to other sentences. One of his devices was the decomposing of sentences into smaller ones. Here is an example, illustrating (very broadly) how a complex sentence can be related to a simpler one by successive operations of stripping material:

1 The attitudes that people in
   T   N   WH   N   P

power express are for public
N   tVn   tVb   P   A

effect
N

2 Attitudes that people
      N   WH   N

express are for effect
tVn   tVb   P   N

3 Attitudes are for effect
     N   tVb P   N

Harris's work was viewed by most of his colleagues as eccentric and extreme, but it did have a deep effect upon one of Harris's students, a young man called Noam Chomsky (b.1928).

Chomsky's Generative Grammar

In the 1950s, Chomsky took Harris's formalist methods and combined them with certain ideas from mathematics, which he had been studying along with linguistics. The result was a strikingly new approach to the description and study of language, and especially of sentence structure (syntax).

> I CALLED MY APPROACH *GENERATIVE GRAMMAR*.

Chomsky introduced his generative ideas in a brief 1957 book, *Syntactic Structures*.

What is Generative Grammar?

A generative grammar of, say, English is an attempt at providing a fully explicit and mechanical statement of the rules governing the construction of English sentences. That is, the rules of the grammar must tell us exactly what can be counted as a grammatical sentence of English, while excluding everything that is not a sentence of English.

> CONSTRUCTING A GENERATIVE GRAMMAR THEREFORE REQUIRES US TO FRAME OUR RULES WITH A DEGREE OF EXPLICITNESS AND ACCURACY NEVER ACHIEVED BY OUR PREDECESSORS.

Here is a brief example of a fragment of a generative grammar of English.

1. S --> NP VP
2. NP --> Det N'
3. N' --> A N
4. N' --> N
5. VP --> V NP

For example, the first rule says "A sentence may consist of a noun phrase followed by a verb phrase". Other rules tell us what a noun phrase can look like, and what a verb phrase can look like. Here are some possible noun phrases:

And here are some possible verb phrases:

These rules are designed to stipulate exactly what can and cannot be a sentence of English. For example, they allow things like

 and

(and also **Posh Spice claws the sofa** and **My cat wants to buy a Porsche**, of course, as these are indeed grammatical sentences of English, if a bit silly).

But they do not allow things like **Destroyed the city our enemies** or **Little the girl her dolly hugged**, which are ungrammatical in English.

Transformational Grammar

There are many different kinds of generative grammar that can be defined, differing in the kinds of rules allowed. The one illustrated on the previous page is a fragment of a context-free phrase-structure grammar, a type which is particularly convenient to work with. But Chomsky himself rejected this kind as too simple to capture important facts about languages.

> *I DEVELOPED INSTEAD A MUCH MORE POWERFUL KIND OF GENERATIVE GRAMMAR, CALLED TRANSFORMATIONAL GRAMMAR, OR TG.*

TG uses enormously powerful rules. For example, to convert

> **The police arrested Susie**

into

> **Susie was arrested by the police**

a single transformational rule does all of the following:

Move **the police** to the end of the sentence.

Insert **by** before **the police**.

Move **Susie** to the beginning of the sentence.

Insert **be** before the verb **arrrested**.

Add tense-marking to convert **be** to **was**. Change the past tense **arrested** to the participle **arrested** (the two forms happen to be identical for *arrest*, but compare **The police took Susie** with **Susie was taken by the police**).

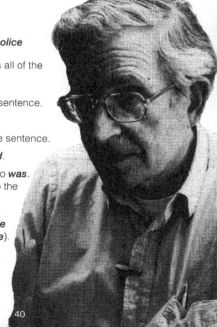

Chomsky's Programme

The point of a good theory of grammar is its *power* to tell us what is possible and impossible in the grammars of human languages. Chomsky himself in the 1950s defined several theories of grammar and ranked them in *order of power*. His point was this.

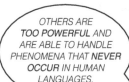

SOME THEORIES OF GRAMMAR ARE TOO FEEBLE AND CANNOT HANDLE CERTAIN PHENOMENA THAT DO OCCUR IN THE GRAMMAR OF HUMAN LANGUAGES.

OTHERS ARE TOO POWERFUL AND ARE ABLE TO HANDLE PHENOMENA THAT NEVER OCCUR IN HUMAN LANGUAGES.

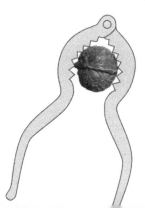

What we want is a good fit: a theory of grammar that can handle exactly the range of grammatical properties found in human languages. When we find such a theory, we will have the best possible theory (or model) of the grammars of human languages.

Paradox of the TG Programme

Chomsky argued that his own theory of *transformational grammar* (TG) provided the best fit. But then, in 1969, the mathematical linguists Stanley Peters and Robert Ritchie proved that TG was so powerful that it could, in principle, describe anything at all that could be described at all –

– hardly an appealing result. But why is this *bad*? Because – to put it simply – it defeats the purpose of a good theory of grammar, which is to tell us what is **possible** and **impossible** in human languages.

A theory that is too powerful is, in effect, claiming that nothing whatever is prohibited in human grammars, and absolutely everything is possible. This is virtually saying that human grammars have *no identifiable properties at all*. In short, TG makes no claim at all!

The Functional Approach

Chomsky and his colleagues have been forced to modify their ideas repeatedly in the face of refractory data. Some critics have been wondering whether the generative enterprise can ever be successfully carried through at all.

For these reasons, among others, many linguists prefer to steer clear of what they see as excessive formalism in favour of more human-centred approaches, approaches that focus far more directly upon what people are trying to do when they speak, and how they go about this task.

One such approach, preferred by many linguists, is the functional approach. These linguists try to determine what purposes are being served by a language, and what linguistic forms are available to serve those functions.

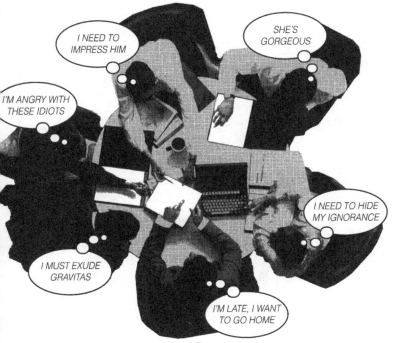

But what do we mean by the functions of language? Most people, on being asked what language is for, provide the same reply: it's for communication. But this answer is far too simple. Consider a rather typical example of genuine language use, recorded in a pub in Birmingham (England). Mick, who has just lost his licence for drinking and driving, and his wife Rita are both talking to a third person, Roy; material in square brackets is not part of the conversation, but has been inserted for clarity.

What Does "Function" Communicate?

Very little information is being communicated here, and that which is being communicated is hardly likely to be essential to the recipient.

What Mick is largely doing is trying to maintain good relations with his friend ...

... while what his wife Rita is doing is largely trying to change Mick's behaviour.

And these goals, maintaining good relations and trying to persuade people to do things, are far more typical of most language use than the bare "passing of facts".

A functionalist approach – and there are quite a few functionalist approaches in use – attaches little importance to determining precisely what is or is not grammatical. Instead, it focuses on the needs of speakers, and looks at linguistic ways of meeting those needs. A functionalist account of the passage quoted above would begin by asking some simple questions:

"What are Mick and Rita trying to do?"

"What devices does English make available for serving those purposes?"

"Why have the speakers chosen the particular devices that they have chosen?"

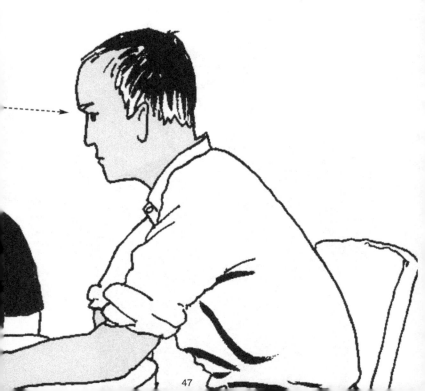

Systemic Functional Linguistics: Texts

One of the most prominent
functional approaches is called
Systemic Functional
Linguistics. This has been
developed by the British
linguist Michael Halliday
(b.1925), and it has become
prominent in Britain and in the
Commonwealth – though
not so far in the USA,
where functional
linguists prefer
somewhat
different
approaches.

SYSTEMIC LINGUISTICS, LIKE
SOME OTHER FUNCTIONAL
APPROACHES, TAKES THE **TEXT** AS THE
PRIMARY UNIT OF ANALYSIS.

Fig. A-1 The 'silver' text

Step 1

// 4 ∧ in / thĭs job / Anne we're // I working with // sìlver //

Step 2

// 1 ∧ now / silver / needs to have / lòve // [// 1 yeà //]
// 3 you / knōw ∧ the // 4 people that / bŭy silver // 1 lòve it //

// 1 yèa // 1 guess they / wòuld //

Step 3

// 1 yèa // 1 mm / ∧ well / natùrally I / mean to / say that it's // 13 got a
/ lovely / gleàm a/bout it you / knōw // 3 ∧ and / if they come /
īn they're // 1 usually / people who / love / beautiful / thìngs //

Step 4

// 1 ∧ so / you / have to be / beautiful / wìth it you / know //
1 ∧ and you / sèll it with / beauty //

// 1 ùm //

Step 5

// 1 ∧ you / ∧ I'm / sùre you know / how to do // 4 thăt // ∧
// 1 oh but you / mùst //

Step 6

// 1 let's hear / ∧ let's hear / ∧ lòok / ∧ you say // 1 màdam //
5 isn't / that / bèautiful //

Step 7

// 4 ∧ if / you sug/gĕst it's beautiful // 1 they / sèe it as / beautiful //

It has developed effective ways of analysing texts – a topic utterly beyond the scope of formalist approaches like Chomsky's, since the rules holding texts together cannot be rigorously formalized in the way that the rules holding sentences together can be.

Cognitive Linguistics

Another and quite different approach which has become prominent only in the last few years is *cognitive linguistics*. Cognitive linguists are interested in understanding the structure and functioning of language in terms of human perception and cognition.

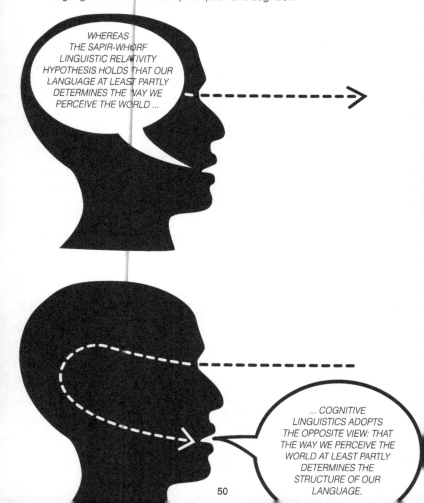

WHEREAS THE SAPIR-WHORF LINGUISTIC RELATIVITY HYPOTHESIS HOLDS THAT OUR LANGUAGE AT LEAST PARTLY DETERMINES THE WAY WE PERCEIVE THE WORLD ...

... COGNITIVE LINGUISTICS ADOPTS THE OPPOSITE VIEW: THAT THE WAY WE PERCEIVE THE WORLD AT LEAST PARTLY DETERMINES THE STRUCTURE OF OUR LANGUAGE.

Gendering Nouns

A prime mover in the development of cognitive linguistics has been the American linguist George Lakoff (b.1941), a former Chomskyan whose interests have changed. In his famous book *Women, Fire and Dangerous Things*, Lakoff draws attention to a curious property of the Australian language Dyirbal, described some years earlier by the British linguist Bob Dixon. Like many European languages, Dyirbal has grammatical gender: that is, each noun must be assigned to one of the available genders. In European languages, the gender of a noun is usually unpredictable from its meaning.

*FOR EXAMPLE, THE GENDER OF THE WORD FOR "TABLE" IS UNPREDICTABLE. THE WORD IS **MASCULINE** IN GERMAN, **FEMININE** IN FRENCH, AND **NEUTER** IN GREEK.*

der Tisch
la table
to trapézi

Dyirbal Noun Genders

Now Dyirbal has four genders, and the gender of a noun usually is predictable from its meaning – but the rules are surprising. For example, one of the four gender classes, called gender class II by Dixon, includes all nouns pertaining to *women*, all those pertaining to *fire*, and all those denoting things that are *dangerous* – poisonous snakes, stinging nettles, and the like.

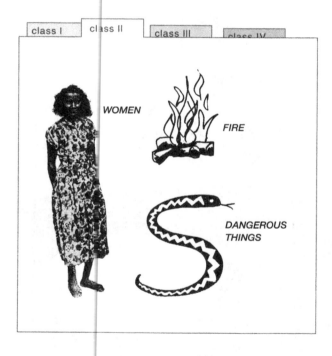

Lakoff was wondering what it is about their perception of the world that induces Dyirbal speakers to assign these words a common gender. The answer here is far from obvious, but cognitive linguists believe that a good deal of language structure can be explained in terms of perception.

Language Perception Differences

Here's an example. In English, when we say that something is in front of us, we often mean that it's in the future, while something which is behind us is in the past. This seems so natural to us that we rarely think about it. But not all languages are the same.

The ancient Greeks did it the other way round.

FOR US, THE FUTURE WAS *BEHIND*, WHILE THE PAST WAS *IN FRONT*.

Greek Perception of Time

The answer appears to lie in the way that people perceive time. We English speakers, apparently, perceive time as standing still while we travel forward through it.

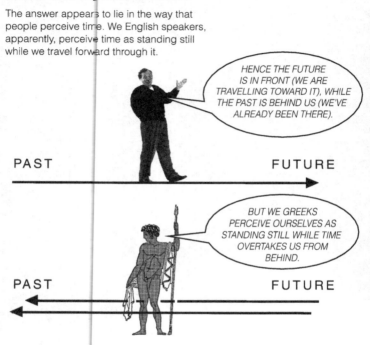

HENCE THE FUTURE IS IN FRONT (WE ARE TRAVELLING TOWARD IT), WHILE THE PAST IS BEHIND US (WE'VE ALREADY BEEN THERE).

PAST   FUTURE

BUT WE GREEKS PERCEIVE OURSELVES AS STANDING STILL WHILE TIME OVERTAKES US FROM BEHIND.

PAST   FUTURE

So, the future was still behind the Greeks – and not yet visible – while the past was already in front of them – and hence visible, at least to some extent.

The striking linguistic differences therefore result from two different ways of perceiving the flow of time: ourselves travelling through time versus time travelling past us. And such perceptual differences, cognitive linguists believe, may show up as differences in language structure, as in this case.

Metaphor

The key notion here is *metaphor*. We and the ancient Greeks have used different metaphors for time, and metaphor – to be precise, cognitive metaphor – plays a central role in much cognitive work.

Here's another cognitive metaphor from English. In English, anger is commonly perceived, metaphorically, as a hot liquid within our bodies. Accordingly, we say things like ...

She's really steamed up

She's boiling

and

She blew her top

Such locutions are incomprehensible without a grasp of the cognitive metaphor on which they are based.

What is Language?

The formalist, functionalist and cognitive approaches are just three of the principal ways in which linguists are trying to get to grips with the rich and complex nature of human languages. Now, so far we have taken it for granted that we know what languages are. But this is not so obvious. We need now to clarify what we mean by the term "language".

Linguistics is the scientific study of language – but what is language? Does the term *language* here include things like ...

... THE LANGUAGE OF FLOWERS?

... THE LANGUAGE OF DANCE?

... THE LANGUAGE OF DOLPHINS?

Does it include made-up languages like Esperanto?

No, it does not.

Natural Language

The term *language* is used by linguists (practitioners of linguistics) in a very specific sense. Let's start with individual languages. An individual language is anything that is, or once was, the mother tongue of a group of human beings. Often linguists use the more explicit term *natural language* for a language in this sense. So, English is a natural language, and so are French, Japanese, Swahili and Pitjantjatjara (spoken in western Australia).

LIKEWISE, SUMERIAN IS A NATURAL LANGUAGE, SINCE IT WAS THE MOTHER TONGUE OF MANY OF THE PEOPLE OF WHAT IS NOW IRAQ, SEVERAL THOUSANDS OF YEARS AGO, EVEN THOUGH IT DIED OUT LONG AGO.

AND SO IS MANX, SPOKEN ON THE ISLE OF MAN UNTIL THE 20TH CENTURY, BUT NOW ALSO EXTINCT.

Our Language Faculty

Now, as we'll see in a bit, all these natural languages have important features in common, so many features that we can regard all of them as variations on a theme. And that common theme is what we call *language*.

OUR *LANGUAGE FACULTY* IS OUR ABILITY TO LEARN AND USE A LANGUAGE.

AND IT'S ONE OF THE CHARACTERISTICS THAT SET HUMAN BEINGS APART FROM ALL OTHER CREATURES ON THE PLANET.

In fact, many people would argue that our unique possession of language is the most important characteristic that we have, the one that most decisively sets us apart from all other species.

It doesn't matter whether a language has a billion speakers (like Mandarin Chinese) or only a tiny handful (like some languages of Australia and the Americas). It doesn't matter whether a language is the chief language of one or more nation-states (like Spanish and Arabic) or whether it is spoken only by an obscure group almost unknown to the outside world (like the Hixkaryana and Wari' languages of Brazil). It doesn't matter whether a language has a long and proud literary tradition (like English and French) or whether it has never been written at all (like most of the world's languages).

ALL THAT MATTERS IS THAT A LANGUAGE SHOULD BE LEARNED IN CHILDHOOD BY A GROUP OF CHILDREN AND THEN USED IN ADULTHOOD, SO THAT IT QUALIFIES AS A NATURAL LANGUAGE.

For linguists, all languages are equal, since they all provide equally good insights into what human languages can be like.

What's Special About Human Languages?

How many languages are there? At present, well over 6,500. We have probably now discovered practically all of the languages that are currently used.

THOUGH A NEW ONE TURNS UP OCCASIONALLY.

OF COURSE, THE TOTAL IS NOT FIXED.

LANGUAGES ARE DYING OUT ALL THE TIME, AS THEIR SPEAKERS ABANDON THEM IN FAVOUR OF OTHER LANGUAGES.

AT THE SAME TIME, NEW LANGUAGES ARE COMING INTO EXISTENCE.

THE BRAZILIAN LANGUAGE PIRAHA WAS DISCOVERED ONLY IN 1995 BY THE AMERICAN LINGUIST DAN EVERETT.

LATER IN THIS BOOK, WE'LL LEARN OF A LANGUAGE THAT WAS BORN ONLY AFTER 1979.

Why are human languages so special? After all, most creatures can communicate in some way with their fellows. Birds sing; crickets chirp; dolphins click; and vervet monkeys have some remarkably specific calls with meanings like ...

LOOK OUT! EAGLE!

Even honeybees have an astoundingly effective system for informing their nestmates about the location and quality of nectar sources.

What do all Languages Have in Common?

Around 1960, the American linguist Charles Hockett (b.1916) began pointing out that all human languages possess a number of striking and important properties that are absent from the signalling systems of all other creatures on the planet. Hockett called these properties the *design features* of language; here are some of them.

All languages have words, and all languages have thousands of words.

THOSE FABLED "PRIMITIVE" LANGUAGES, CONSISTING OF 200 WORDS SUPPLEMENTED BY GRUNTS AND GESTURES, DO NOT EXIST.

NO OTHER CREATURES APPEAR TO HAVE WORDS.

All languages have devices for acquiring new words as required:

CD-ROM, Trekkie, trainspotter, AIDS, soundbite, hyperthermophile

No other creatures can do this.

All languages have ways of modifying the meanings of words:

take, took, have taken, is taking, will be taken.

No other creatures can do this.

All languages have negation:

**Susie smokes;
Susie doesn't smoke.**

But negation is unique to us: a dog can say ...

All languages can form questions:

Does Susie smoke?

All languages permit abstractions like

redness, curvature and **absence.**

All languages permit displacement, the ability to talk about things other than the here and now:

I was in Paris last week.

I want to be an astronomer when I grow up.

What do you suppose the surface of Venus is like?

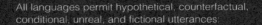

All languages permit hypothetical, counterfactual, conditional, unreal, and fictional utterances:

Legolas the elf quietly drew his sword.

Europeans could not survive in the Australian desert.

If I spoke better French, I could get a job in Paris.

If you'll cook the quiche, I'll make the salad.

All languages exhibit *open-endedness*, the ability to produce and understand totally new utterances without difficulty:

Luxembourg has invaded New Zealand.

Shakespeare wrote his plays in Swahili, and they were translated into English by his African bodyguards.

Aunt Bea has sent us some photos of her granddaughter's christening.

I find that peanut butter is a poor substitute for putty.

Very likely most of the sentences in this book are ones that you have never used or encountered before, and yet you can still understand them easily.

All languages exhibit *stimulus-freedom*, the ability to say anything at all, including nothing, in any circumstance. If your friend Julia asks you ...

... you can make any reply you like:

Linguistic Abilities

No other creatures can do these things. But all humans can: an Oxford professor or a Chicago stockbroker can do them effortlessly, but so can a Stone Age tribesman in New Guinea or the Amazon, and so can a seven-year-old child in Siberia. Language is peculiarly human ...

Language Media

Language must be expressed through a *medium*. A *primary medium* is one in which a mother tongue can be acquired, and there are just two primary media. The more familiar one is *speech*. In speech, air from the lungs is squeezed up and out through the mouth and the nose, while the vocal folds, the tongue and other organs of speech modify the airstream in various ways to produce a sequence of speech sounds representing larger linguistic units like words and sentences.

The other one is *signing*, in which language is expressed as a series of signs – gestures – made chiefly with the hands, the head, the face and the upper body.

SIGN LANGUAGES ARE MAINLY USED BY DEAF PEOPLE WHO CANNOT HEAR SPEECH.

Units of Writing

There are also *secondary media*, in which language is transferred from a primary medium to another one. Most familiar here is *writing*, in which a spoken or signed language is converted into permanent marks on a solid surface. But no language can be written down until its speakers have first analysed it into certain recurrent units, for each of which a written symbol can be provided. There are several possible ways of doing this, but the most widely used approach today is an *alphabet*, in which each written character represents – in principle, at least – a single basic sound unit.

Ancient Phoenician alphabet

Modern Hebrew alphabet

Modern Arabic alphabet

70

Every spoken language contains a small number of basic sound units, or phonemes. Among the phonemes of English are /k/, /æ/ and /t/. If we produce these phonemes in the order /kæt/, we get the word *cat*. But the order /tæk/ gives us *tack*, while /ækt/ yields *act*, /æt/ gives *at*, and /tækt/ gives *tact* or *tacked* (which are pronounced identically, in spite of their different structures).

The individual phonemes are meaningless: it makes no sense to ask what /k/ or /æ/ means in English. But particular combinations like /kæt/ and /tæk/ are highly meaningful.

71

Duality of Patterning

This is the way every spoken language is built up. A small number of meaningless phonemes can be combined into meaningful sequences, such as words. We call this arrangement *duality of patterning*, and duality is unique to human languages.

What could we do if we didn't have duality? Well, every different sound would have to have its own meaning attached. But we can't produce many more than about a hundred easily distinguishable speech sounds.

> SO WITHOUT DUALITY, OUR LANGUAGES COULD HAVE ONLY ABOUT A HUNDRED DIFFERENT MEANINGFUL "WORDS" – NOT NEARLY ENOUGH FOR OUR PURPOSES.

But this is exactly what non-human species do. They operate with "one-sound-one-meaning" – and so they can produce only a few different meanings: usually three to six, maybe twenty or so at most. This is one major reason why we can say a limitless number of different things, while other creatures can't. An animal can only ever choose one from a very short list of possible things to "say". A monkey can say ...

LOOK OUT – DANGER IN THE AIR!

... if that message is available in the system, but it can't come out with the slightest novelty, such as "Look out – two hunters with rifles!"

Sign Languages

Sign languages are a little different here. The
number of possible signs is very much larger
than the number of possible speech sounds.
Even so, every sign can be decomposed into a
small number of meaningless elements such as
hand position, direction and speed of
movement, and other body-parts touched.

British Sign
Language
(BSL)

Sign languages, by the way, are not crude or derivative systems. A sign language is a real language, just like English or Spanish. A sign language can be acquired by a child as its first language. A sign language has a large vocabulary and a rich and elaborate system of grammar: breaking a rule of grammar is just as bad in a sign language as it is in a spoken language.

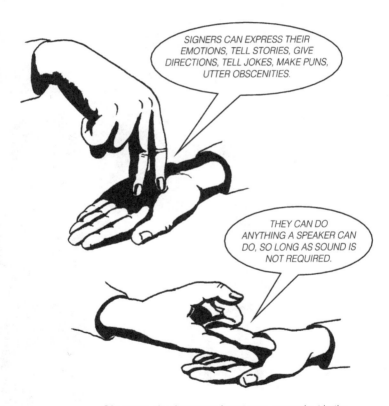

SIGNERS CAN EXPRESS THEIR EMOTIONS, TELL STORIES, GIVE DIRECTIONS, TELL JOKES, MAKE PUNS, UTTER OBSCENITIES.

THEY CAN DO ANYTHING A SPEAKER CAN DO, SO LONG AS SOUND IS NOT REQUIRED.

Of course, sign language is not very convenient in the dark, but then spoken language is not very convenient in ear-splitting noise – no problem for signers.

Nicaraguan Sign Language

As it happens, the world's newest known natural language is a sign language. After the 1979 revolution in Nicaragua, the new government collected the hundreds of deaf children who had been brutally shut away under the old regime and brought them together in a special school. Remarkably, within a short time the deaf children began to construct a brand-new sign language.

WE USED IT AMONG OURSELVES.

SOON WE WERE TEACHING IT TO NEW ARRIVALS.

Nicaragua

These children became the first-ever native users of Nicaraguan Sign Language (NSL), as the language is now called. Today, NSL, which did not exist in any form in 1979, has some hundreds of native users.

Grammar and Word Order

One of the most important properties of language is *grammar*. Grammar is a set of rules for combining words into sentences, for modifying the forms of the words for particular purposes, and for interpreting the result. Every language has a grammar – indeed, every language has quite a lot of grammar. There is no such thing as a language with little or no grammar. But the rules of grammar differ from language to language.

Take word order. In English, the only normal order in sentences is *subject-verb-object*, or SVO, as in ...

Mike washed the car

Mike
is the subject

washed
is the verb

the car
is the object

But other languages may be different.

Different Examples of Word Order and Location

Irish is VSO, and an Irish-speaker says, literally,

Washed / Mike / the car.

Japanese is SOV, and a Japanese-speaker says

Mike / the car / washed.

Malagasy (in Madagascar) is VOS, and the result is

Washed / the car / Mike.

Hixkaryana, in Brazil, is OVS, and so we get

The car / washed / Mike.

In these languages, the English order would be just as wrong as the other orders are in English.

Or consider location in space. In English, we express this by putting a little grammatical word before the name of the place, as in

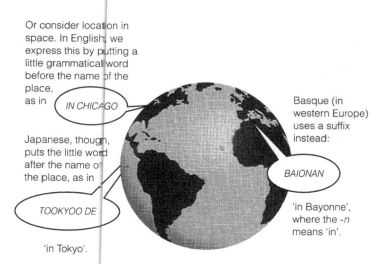

IN CHICAGO

Japanese, though, puts the little word after the name of the place, as in

TOOKYOO DE

'in Tokyo'.

Basque (in western Europe) uses a suffix instead:

BAIONAN

'in Bayonne', where the -n means 'in'.

Tense and Time

Or consider tense, the grammatical marking of time. In English, we have only a single past-tense form: I say *I saw John*, regardless of whether I saw him ten minutes ago or ten years ago. But some other languages make finer distinctions. In European Spanish, you must say *Le he visto a Juan* if you saw John earlier today, but *Le vi a Juan* if you saw him before today. In the New Guinea language Yimas, there are four different past-tense forms, all distinguishing different degrees of remoteness in the past.

And in the African language Bamileke-Dschang, there are five. On the other hand, Chinese has no tense-marking at all: there is nothing corresponding to the difference between *see* and *saw*.

Grammatical Differences

In English, if we want to refer to somebody or something we've already mentioned, we must choose among *he* for a male, *she* for a female and *it* for a sexless thing. In this case, English grammaticalizes sex.

In Finnish, however, the word is *hän* in every case: Finnish does not mark sex.

Basque, in northern Spain, does not mark sex either, but in Basque you must make a different choice: *hau* if the person or thing is close to you, *hori* if an intermediate distance from you, and *hura* if far away from you. Basque grammaticalizes distance, but not sex.

In the North American language Kwakiutl, you must make yet another choice: you choose one form if you can see the person or thing you're talking about, but another form if you can't. Kwakiutl grammaticalizes visibility.

In standard English, the sentence *He's sick* can mean either "He's sick at the moment" or "He's chronically ill". If we need to make the difference, we have to stick extra words into the sentence. However, in one variety of English, African-American English (AAE), spoken by many black people in the USA, the difference is grammaticalized.

The rules of English grammar are not the same for all speakers.

Sign Language Grammar

In American Sign Language, the sign for sick can be grammatically modified in a number of ways, producing variations that mean "slightly sick", "very sick", "always sick", "sick for a long time", and several other possibilities, all of which require extra words in English. Sign languages, like spoken languages, have rich and elaborate grammatical systems.

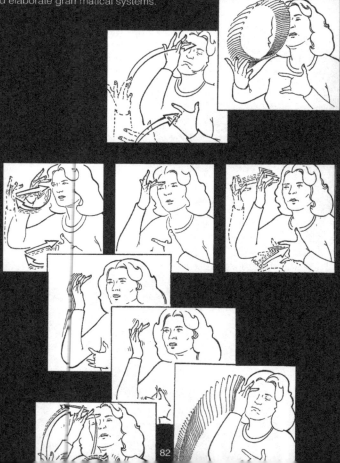

Our remarkable language faculty is unique to our species. But when did language arise? No one knows.

50,000 years ago

100,000 years ago

200,000 years ago

1,000,000 years ago

*THE FAVOURITE GUESS IS THAT LANGUAGE AROSE WITH OUR OWN SPECIES, **HOMO SAPIENS**, BETWEEN 100,000 AND 200,000 YEARS AGO.*

*BUT A FEW SPECIALISTS ARE ARGUING THAT OUR HOMINID ANCESTOR, **HOMO ERECTUS**, PROBABLY HAD LANGUAGE AROUND A MILLION YEARS AGO.*

WHILE STILL OTHERS BELIEVE THAT OUR OWN SPECIES FIRST ACQUIRED LANGUAGE ONLY AROUND 50,000 YEARS AGO.

No resolution to this debate is in sight. Sadly, languages do not fossilize.

The Written Record of Language

Investigation of our remote linguistic past is very difficult. For one thing, writing was invented only a little more than 5,000 years ago, and we have no written records earlier than this. In fact, until recently, only a tiny proportion of the world's people could read and write, and even today only a few dozen languages are regularly written. Most languages have never been written down at all, and so we have no record of the overwhelming bulk of the world's linguistic history.

But writing changes too

Languages are always changing, not just century by century but day by day. Take a look at this passage written by Jonathan Swift in the 18th century:

> But where I say, that I would have our Language, after it is duly correct, always to last; I do not mean that it should never be enlarged: Provided, that no Word which a Society shall give a Sanction to, be afterwards antiquated and exploded, they may have liberty to receive whatever new ones they shall find occasion for.

We can understand most of this, but it already looks strange to us.

My brother Jacques he keeps at school, and
report speaks goldenly of his profit; for my part,
he keeps me rustically at home, or, to speak
more properly, stays me here at home unkept;
for call you that keeping for a gentleman of my
birth, that differs not from the stalling of an ox?

This is a little more
difficult, and even
stranger, but still mostly
comprehensible in
writing.

*THOUGH IF YOU COULD HEAR
ME SPEAK, YOU WOULD FIND ME VERY
HARD TO UNDERSTAND, MAYBE
IMPOSSIBLE.*

And Further Back ...

Now look at a passage from Chaucer, in the 14th century:

> A yong man whilom called Melibeus myghty
> and riche bigat vp on his wif, that called was
> Prudence a doghter, which that called was
> Sophie. Vpon a day bifel that he for his desport
> is went into the feeldes hym to pleye.

This is on the very brink of
incomprehensibility in writing.

*AND MY SPEECH, IF YOU
COULD HEAR IT, WOULD BE
UTTERLY INCOMPREHENSIBLE
TO YOU.*

We could no more
understand Chaucer's
spoken English than we can
understand spoken Dutch.

... to Old English

Finally, look at a sample of English from the 10th century, during the period we call Old English:

Her...Ælfred cyning...gefeaht with ealne here, and hine geflymde, and him aefter rad oth thet geweorc, and thaer saet XIII niht.

['Here King Alfred fought against the whole army, and put it to flight, and rode after it to the fortress, and there he camped for thirteen nights.']

This time even the written version is completely beyond us. Indeed, you might find it hard to believe that this passage is in English at all. But it is, though hardly our sort of English. During the last thousand years, English has changed out of all recognition.

The Never-ending Story

Now, a thousand years is only about forty generations, but, all
during those *forty generations*, the language has been
changing: a new pronunciation here, a new word there, a new
grammatical form somewhere else, and – well, you see the
result. Language change is ceaseless and remorseless, and it
causes languages to diverge from their earlier forms almost
without limit.

This change never stops. Utterances like ...

*I LOGGED ONTO THE
WEB WITH MY LAPTOP AND
ASKED MY SEARCH ENGINE TO
FIND HER HOME PAGE.*

... would have been
incomprehensible gibberish
only a few years ago. But
languages don't change
merely because the world
changes. A popular
magazine can write this ...

"After all those ditzy
bimbos, I thought I'd be a
wuss to pass up this
stonking part, even if it is
an indie flick", she said.

... also incomprehensible a
few years ago.

My nieces and my nephew grew up in the same area as I did, but about 30 years later. Already their English is a little different from mine: some different words, a few different usages, and a noticeably different pronunciation, especially in the vowels. Occasionally I have a little trouble understanding them. This is one more generation of change, piled onto all those generations of change that came before.

These constant changes often attract the ire of linguistic conservatives. Furious letters get written to newspapers complaining about usages that the writers did not grow up with:

Hopefully, we'll be there in time for lunch.

We have **less** students than we did last year.

Who do you trust?

This one is different **to** the others.

I'm bored **of** boy bands.

– and countless others.

Conservative Prescriptivism

But this is nothing new. Two hundred years ago, the construction illustrated by *My house is being painted* did not exist in standard English, and the only possible form was *My house is painting*. When a few innovating speakers began to say things like *My house is being painted*, the linguistic conservatives of the day could not contain their fury, and they attacked the new form as ...

CONFUSING!

ILLOGICAL!

MONSTROUS!

MY HOUSE IS PAINTING

Well, you can see just how effective their protests were: today everybody says "My house is being painted", and nobody would now dream of trying to get away with the defunct older form.

This conservative attitude is called *prescriptivism,* and it is a powerful force in almost any society, but especially in one with a written tradition, such as ours. Educated people, by definition, have acquired a command of the standard language of their day, especially the written standard, and they are often deeply reluctant to accept any changes into the language they have grown up with and learned in school. But, as the examples cited above show, many or most of these changes pass into the language anyway, and eventually become accepted as part of the modified standard language. Those who reject the changes, and rail against them, eventually die, and the only speakers left are those who have grown up with the newer forms and regard them as normal. These younger speakers may rail in turn against the next set of changes, but again to no avail. They too will die and leave the field to the next generation of speakers, who accept yet further innovations. Thus it goes on for ever.

Historical Perspectives

In fact, though, prescriptivists do not always complain only about changes. For example, many speakers of British English complain about what they see as "Americanisms" invading their speech, such as *I guess* for *I suppose* and *I've just gotten a letter* for *I've just got a letter*.

BUT THEY DON'T REALIZE THAT THESE "AMERICAN" FORMS IN FACT ORIGINATED IN BRITAIN AND CROSSED THE ATLANTIC TO AMERICA ...

... after which they largely died out in Britain. Prescriptivism at its worst is no more than hostility to the unfamiliar.

For English, we have written texts extending back about 1,200 years, and so we can watch the changes in the language unfolding in our texts. Before that time, though, English was not being written down, and it becomes much more difficult to figure out what was happening.

Difficult, but not impossible, because we have another way of getting at linguistic prehistory – at least when we are lucky, and we are lucky here. Look at the table below, showing a few words of similar meaning in English, Swedish and German.

	English	Swedish	German
(a)	tooth	tand	Zahn
	two	tva	zwei
	ten	tio	zehn
(b)	three	tre	drei
	thing	ting	Ding
	thick	tjock	dick
(c)	nine	nio	neun
	new	ny	neu
	night	natt	Nacht

Now, you may notice a few striking similarities among some of these words, but the similarities are not the point at all. What is important is the *patterns* on view. In word after word, when an English word starts with /t/, the corresponding Swedish word starts with / **t** /, while the corresponding German word starts with / **ts** / (spelled *z*). Likewise, when an English word starts with / θ / (spelled *th*), the corresponding Swedish word starts with / **t** /, and the German one with / **d** /. And, when the English word starts with / **n** /, the Swedish one has / **n** / and the German one / **n** /.

Such patterns are called *systemic correspondences*, and there are many such correspondences linking these three languages, as well as some other languages.

Explaining Systemic Correspondence

How can we explain these systemic correspondences? There is really only one way. Once, long ago, these three languages were the same language! We call this ancestral language *Proto-Germanic*. The speakers of Proto-Germanic could not write, and so we have no records of it, but we can still figure out quite a bit about it, and about what happened to it. Proto-Germanic was probably spoken in southern Scandinavia around 500 BC. From there its speakers began spreading out over much of northern Europe. As they spread, of course, their language continued to change, but it didn't change everywhere in the same way. Instead, different changes happened in different places, and so the original language gradually split up into regional varieties which became ever more different from one another.

English

Frisian

Proto-Germanic

Dutch

Flemish

German   Yiddish

Afrikaans

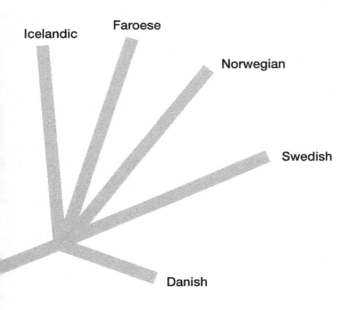

But the changes in pronunciation were rather regular. All the words in group (a) shown on page 93 started in Proto-Germanic with the same sound, which turned into /t/ in English and Swedish but into /ts/ in German. Likewise, all the words in group (b) started with the same sound, which became /θ/ in English, /t/ in Swedish and /d/ in German, and similarly for group (c). The combination of language change with time and geographical separation has not only changed the original language beyond recognition, it has broken that language up into a number of quite distinct *daughter* languages. Apart from English, Swedish and German, the daughters of Proto-Germanic include Icelandic, Faroese, Norwegian, Danish, Dutch, Afrikaans, Yiddish, and a number of extinct languages like Gothic. We call these the *Germanic* languages, and the Germanic languages constitute a *family* of languages – that is, a group of related languages all descended from a single common ancestor.

The Indo-European Family and PIE

And Proto-Germanic is not the end of the story, or rather it is not the beginning. Two hundred years ago, to their own astonishment, European linguists began to realize that Germanic itself forms just one modest branch of a much vaster family of languages. That family has been named the *Indo-European* family, and it includes, besides Germanic, the Celtic languages like Irish and Welsh, Latin and its Romance descendants like Spanish, French and Italian, the Slavic languages like Polish and Russian, Albanian, Greek, Armenian, the Iranian languages like Persian and Kurdish, the Indic languages like Hindi, Urdu and Bengali, and a number of long-extinct languages once spoken in places like Turkey and Chinese Turkestan.

Naturally, the Indo-European languages are all descended from a remote common ancestor called *Proto-Indo-European* (PIE), which we think was spoken around 6,000 years ago, somewhere in eastern Europe or western Asia, by people who of course left no written records. The establishment of the Indo-European family was the great achievement of the linguists of the 19th century.

Old Prussian — Baltic
Lithuanian
Latvian — West Slavic
Polish
Slovak — South Slavic
Czech   Slovene
Serbo Croatian   Macedonian
Bulgarian

Icelandic
Faroese
Norwegian
Swedish
Danish
English — Old German
Frisian
Dutch
Flemish — Yiddish
Afrikaans   German

Irish Gaelic — Goidelic
Scottish Gaelic   Manx — Brythonic
Welsh
Cornish   Breton — Gaulish
— Latino-Faliscan
Portuguese   Latin
Spanish
Catalan — Faliscan
Provençal
French — Rumanian
Italian   Rhaeto-Romance

The Remote Origins of English

This is as far back as we can trace the prehistory of English. Somewhere around 6,000 years ago, an illiterate people somewhere in Eurasia began to spread out from their homeland. Eventually, around 3,000 years ago, some of them entered Scandinavia, where their speech developed into Proto-Germanic. The speakers of this language then spread southward into much of northern Europe, where their language began breaking up into a number of distinct regional varieties. One group moved into the North Sea coast of the Continent, where their speech developed into a collection of local varieties we call *Ingvaeonic*. After the Roman retreat from Britain, some of these Ingvaeonic speakers moved into Britain, where their speech gradually diverged from that of their relatives back home, until finally it was so different that it had to be regarded as a different language. And that language is the ancestor of our own English.

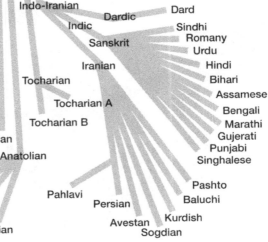

PIE

Balto-Slavic
East Slavic
Russian
krainian
Byelorussian
Proto-Germanic
orth Germanic
West Germanic
ast Germanic
othic
Celtic
Illyrian
Italic
Albanian
Osco-Umbrian
Thracian
Umbrian
Hellenic
Oscan
Armenian
Greek
Phrygian
Anatolian
Hittite
Luvian
Lycian
Lydian
Indo-Iranian
Dardic
Indic
Sanskrit
Iranian
Tocharian
Tocharian A
Tocharian B
Pahlavi
Persian
Avestan
Sogdian
Kurdish
Dard
Sindhi
Romany
Urdu
Hindi
Bihari
Assamese
Bengali
Marathi
Gujerati
Punjabi
Singhalese
Pashto
Baluchi

Eastern Ancestors of PIE

And what came before PIE? Clearly, PIE must itself have been descended from a still earlier ancestor, and so we might hope to go on finding ever more distant relatives for English somewhere on the globe. But this is hard. The further back in time we go, the greater the weight of accumulated changes we have to decipher, the fuzzier and blurrier becomes our picture of the linguistic facts, and the more distant and difficult to identify become any relatives that might be out there.

At present, no relatives for Indo-European have been identified. Several linguists have been intrigued by a possible link with the neighbouring *Uralic* family, which includes Finnish and Hungarian, among others.

Others, far more ambitious, are trying hard to find evidence that Indo-European and Uralic are both distantly related to a startling collection of Eurasian language families, including Turkic, Mongolic, Tungusic (in Siberia), Dravidian (in southern India), Kartvelian (in the Caucasus), the huge Afro-Asiatic family of the Near East (which includes Arabic and Hebrew, among others), and perhaps still more; this proposal is called the Nostratic hypothesis. But the evidence available to support these ideas is too tiny to persuade most linguists that we are looking at anything more than chance resemblances. We may never find a relative for Indo-European, even if some other living families really are very remotely related to it. Thousands of years of language change is just too effective at obliterating the remaining traces of a language's ancestry. Given enough time, everything changes.

The Saussurean Paradox

And this brings us to a famous issue in linguistics, known as the *Saussurean paradox*. How can we continue to speak a language effectively while it is *constantly changing*? After all, how could we play chess or football if the rules were constantly changing during a match?

AND HOW COULD WE TRY A CASE IN COURT IF THE LAW WERE CONSTANTLY CHANGING DURING THE TRIAL?

Well, there is a clue in that sentence:

... if the law **were** constantly changing ...

Long ago, English had a complete set of distinctive verb-forms for talking about hypothetical states of affairs, the *subjunctive*. Most of these forms disappeared long ago, but a few cling to the edges of the language, including the one shown in *if it **were***. You may or may not use this form, but you probably at least recognize it. It continues to exist in the language, even though most people now say *if the law **was** constantly changing*. Some people say *were* all the time in this construction; some say *was* all the time but understand *were*; and some people vary, using *were* in some circumstances but *was* in others.

Variation

The key here is *variation*. Both forms, *were* and *was,* exist side by side in English, and both are used and understood. Once upon a time, everybody said *were*. And one day in the future, everybody will say *was*. Meanwhile, we have variation. And variation, we now understand, is the vehicle of change. When a change is in progress, the older form and the newer form coexist, and almost everybody is familiar with both forms, even if some people use only one or the other. Over time, the older form becomes less and less frequent, and the newer one becomes ever more frequent, until, one day, there is no one left alive still using the older form, and the change is complete.

So, for example, before the Norman Conquest of England, all English-speakers said *here* for "army". Some time after the Conquest, a few people began to use the Norman French word *army* when speaking English. For a long time, the two words coexisted in English. But more and more people began to use *army* in preference to *here,* and finally a day came when there was no one left saying *here* at all, and the word became extinct. Today this old word survives only in a few place-names, such as *Hereford* in England ("army-ford"), and no one except a specialist any longer knows what this name means.

Sociolinguistic Studies of Variation

We can choose between *telephone* and *phone*, between *gymnasium* and *gym*, between *omnibus* and *bus*, between *brassière* and *bra*, and after a while one form is no longer used at all – as has now happened with *omnibus*, and perhaps also with *brassière*.

The study of variation in language is *sociolinguistics*, and the sociolinguists are interested in more than language change. For example, they are interested in the speech of *men* and *women*. In some languages, men and women speak very differently: they use different pronunciations, different words, and even different grammatical endings.

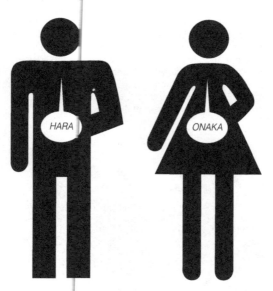

Among speakers of Japanese, "stomach" is *hara* among men but *onaka* among women. Among speakers of Koasati in Louisiana, "lift it!" is *lakawhol* when women speak but *lakawhos* when men speak.

English has nothing quite like this, but we too have our sex differences in speech. For a woman, a particular jumper is *burgundy*, while for a man it is only *red*. For a woman, it is normal to say *That's a wonderful tunic you're wearing, Susie*, while, for a man, saying ...

... is in most circumstances quite unacceptable.

An important difference between men's and women's speech has been uncovered only recently by the British linguist Jennifer Coates. Coates has studied all-male and all-female conversations, and found some striking differences.

Male-versus-Female Speech

In all-male conversations, men engage in
floor-holding.

But women don't do this at all. Instead, while one woman is speaking, the others constantly chip in with supporting contributions, ranging from "That's right!" to completing the speaker's sentence for her.

This difference, naturally, leads to confusion in mixed-sex conversations. While her male partner is speaking, a woman constantly chips in with supporting remarks, in the usual female style. But the man, who is not used to this, will very likely interpret these remarks as interruptions – which they are not – and become very annoyed. This is probably why so many men sincerely believe that women interrupt all the time – whereas, in fact, observation shows that, in mixed-sex conversations, it is men who do most of the interrupting.

Variation and Social Context

Variation is pervasive in language. Men don't speak like women. Plumbers don't speak like stockbrokers. Londoners don't speak like Glaswegians. Students don't speak like retired colonels. Disc jockeys don't speak like newsreaders. Everywhere we look, we find endless variation.

Even a single person speaks differently in different circumstances. With your friends in a pub, you might excuse yourself by saying "Gotta pee" – but you wouldn't do the same while chatting politely to your mother's elderly friends, or when being interviewed for a job with a bank. You wouldn't write an essay or a report in the same way that you'd write a personal letter to your lover. And the people who make announcements over supermarket PA systems seem to fall back on a variety of English unknown to the rest of the population.

We **would** liketoinform **all** ourcustomers that **all** roastchickensare **now** selling for **half** priceatour **delica** tessen counter. **Than** kyou.

This variation extends not only over social groups and contexts, but also over both time and place. At various times, in various places, and in various contexts, something exceptionally good has been described within our lifetimes as *ace, top-hole, spiffing, triff, tremendous, excellent, super, jolly good, awesome, smashing, wicked, fab, bodacious, unreal,* and in countless other ways.

One of the most striking things about our use of language is our ability to express meanings that are not really there. Suppose several of us are planning to go to a Christmas party, and we are discussing who should drive. One person remarks ...

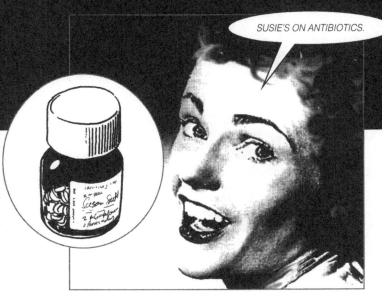

SUSIE'S ON ANTIBIOTICS.

What is the point of this seemingly irrelevant comment? Well, of course it is not irrelevant at all. In the context, it means "Susie can drive". Why? Because, with our experience of the world, we know that Christmas parties involve a lot of drinking, that people who drink cannot safely drive, and that people on antibiotics are usually not allowed to drink. So, in our example, Susie is a good choice of driver.

That is, in our context, the utterance *Susie's on antibiotics* is interpreted to mean *Susie is the obvious person to drive*. Now, this is strange. Clearly, *Susie's on antibiotics* doesn't really have this meaning. But we interpret the utterance in this way anyhow, because of our knowledge of the world.

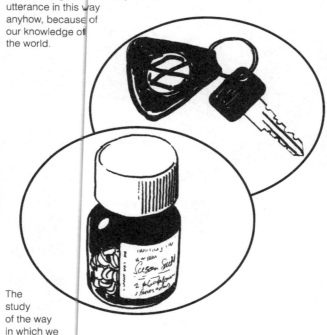

The study of the way in which we extract communicative meanings from the context of utterances is now called *pragmatics*. We distinguish pragmatics from *semantics*, the study of meanings derived entirely from linguistic forms. Let us consider briefly the different approaches of semantics and pragmatics in the next pages.

Semantics

There are aspects of meaning that are intrinsic to linguistic *forms* and not merely dependent on *context*. The study of these intrinsic aspects of meaning is called *semantics*. Semantics is a surprisingly difficult topic to investigate.

Take our familiar word **dog**. Can you write a definition of *dog* which will be adequate to distinguish every dog from every non-dog? This is not so easy. Suppose we try this.

A dog is a four-legged animal with fur, long ears and a tail; it barks, eats meat, and lives with people.

Fine. But the Mexican hairless has no fur: is it therefore not a dog? The basenji cannot bark, yet we still call it a dog. A wild dog doesn't live with people: is it therefore a different species? No? Then why are foxes and wolves not dogs? These creatures are pretty doglike, and the fox even barks. Is a photograph of a dog still a dog? A dead dog? A stuffed dog? A cartoon dog?

AM I NOT A DOG?

It appears that we can't define even such a simple word as *dog* in a rigorous way. Somehow we still seem to know what the word means and use it without difficulty. And, if *dog* is hard, what about defining *small, green, evasive, democracy* and *pornography*? It almost seems a wonder that we can talk to one another at all.

109

Meanings Occur in Connections

But words don't have meaning only in isolation. Much of
their meaning comes from the way they are connected to
other words. Consider the meanings of the words *took
off*, *ran out of* and *lost* in the following examples:

**Susie took her coat off.
Susie took her coat off the
peg.**

**Natalie ran out of the room.
Natalie ran out of flour.**

**Alice lost her toothbrush.
Alice lost her virginity.**

Clearly, the meanings we assign to words depend in
important ways on the meanings of the other words they
occur with. It is facts like these that make
semantics such a difficult study to pursue. Indeed, in
the 1940s, the American structuralists became so
exasperated with the whole messy business of
meaning that they effectively excommunicated
semantics from the field of linguistics for a while –
though it was accepted back into the fold in the 1960s.

Pragmatics

The term *pragmatics* was coined by the American philosopher C.S. Peirce (1839–1914). But it was only in the 1930s that another American philosopher, Charles Morris (1901–79), began to apply the term to aspects of language *behaviour*.

Morris's understanding of the term was very broad and encompassed many aspects of social and psychological behaviour. This broad sense is still usual in Europe today, where pragmatics has at times been understood to include even the study of *beliefs* underlying linguistic behaviour.

In the English-speaking world, though, the application of the term has been steadily narrowed down to the study of meanings derived from the *contexts* of utterances, as opposed to meanings contained within linguistic forms. As a result, linguists and philosophers have come to understand that there are two kinds of linguistic meaning, and two different approaches required to understand them.

Semantics treats the meaning of language as contained within linguistic form.

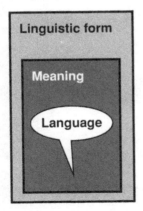

Pragmatics treats the meaning of language as contained within its context.

Pragmatic Issues

Meanwhile, philosophers were looking into pragmatic issues without using the term. In the first half of the 20th century, the British philosophers Bertrand Russell (1872–1970) and Peter Strawson (b.1919) engaged in a debate over the sentence ...

The King of France is bald.

What happens when there is no King of France?

> SINCE THE SENTENCE CANNOT BE TRUE, IT MUST BE SIMPLY FALSE.

> IT MAKES NO SENSE TO ASK WHETHER THIS SENTENCE IS TRUE OR FALSE. WHEN THERE IS NO KING, AN UTTERANCE OF THIS FORM IS SIMPLY INAPPROPRIATE, OUTSIDE THE NORMS OF NORMAL LINGUISTIC BEHAVIOUR.

Strawson's view has been very influential in allowing linguists to develop the view that meaning cannot be wholly understood without reference to context.

Extending Pragmatics

In the 1960s, the British philosopher Paul Grice made groundbreaking contributions to pragmatics when he proposed a set of rules, or *maxims,* governing the structure of conversations. One of these is the maxim of **relevance**, by which we assume that anything we hear is intended to be a relevant contribution to the discussion.

In the example cited above, when we ask for a driver and hear "Susie's on antibiotics", we take it for granted that this response is meant to be a *relevant contribution*, and we interpret it accordingly, drawing for the purpose on our whole breadth of experience and background knowledge. We do this sort of thing all the time, and we scarcely ever notice that we are doing it.

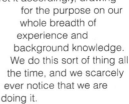

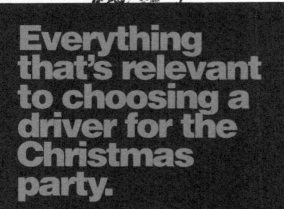

Everything that's relevant to choosing a driver for the Christmas party.

Two more of Grice's maxims are those of **quality** and **quantity**.
Suppose I say to you ...

> **I have two children.**

By **quality**, you will conclude that I do not have *no* children or
one child, since in that case I would be violating the maxim of
quality. Or, in plain English, I would be lying.

By **quantity**, you will conclude that I have exactly *two*
children, and not three or four. If I say this
when I have three children, then I am
not strictly lying, but I am certainly
being uncooperative.

In Grice's analysis, you will
assume that I am cooperating,
that I am obeying the maxim of
quantity, and hence that I have
exactly two children.

> **I accept that
> you are telling the
> truth, and the
> whole truth.**

Where Does Language Come From?

But how does language get into our brains in the first place? In the remote past, people were often inclined to believe that there must be a "natural" human language, which infants left to their own devices would automatically start speaking, without coaching. The Egyptian pharaoh Psammetichus and the English King James I, among others, conducted barbarous experiments.

SUPPOSE I RAISE NEWBORN INFANTS IN ISOLATION. MAYBE THOSE CHILDREN WILL "NATURALLY" BEGIN SPEAKING ENGLISH.

In fact, these poor children learned no language at all.

We now know that a child raised in isolation will never learn a language. Contact with other people is essential in acquiring a first language. But this knowledge doesn't tell us how acquisition occurs.

Skinner's Thesis Attacked by Chomsky

In 1957, the American behavioural psychologist B. F. Skinner published *Verbal Behavior*, a book arguing that children acquire their first language by trying to imitate the adult speech they hear around them. In Skinner's view, acquisition proceeds by a process of imitation and reinforcement.

A GOOD IMITATION OF ADULT SPEECH IS REWARDED WITH PRAISE AND SMILES, WHILE A BAD ONE IS DISCOURAGED BY CORRECTIONS AND FROWNS.

GRADUALLY, THEREFORE, THE CHILD IS PUSHED TOWARD BETTER AND BETTER APPROXIMATIONS TO ADULT SPEECH, UNTIL FINALLY IT IS SPEAKING JUST LIKE AN ADULT.

SKINNER'S VIEW IS **WRONG** – HOPELESSLY WILDLY **WRONG**.

Skinner's book was scathingly, even savagely, reviewed by the then young and unknown Noam Chomsky. And with good reason. Several decades of careful study have now revealed a good deal about the way children acquire their first language, and it turns out that acquisition is utterly different from what Skinner conjectured.

116

Children Construct Rules

If Skinner were right, then children should produce more or less random approximations to adult speech, and they should make more or less random errors. But this is not what happens. Dozens of studies have shown us that children go about the business of language acquisition in a very orderly way. They do not produce random approximations to adult speech, and they do not make random errors.

INSTEAD, THEY DO SOMETHING UTTERLY DIFFERENT.

WE CONSTRUCT RULES.

Consider English past tenses. Most English verbs form regular past tenses: *love / loved, wash / washed, smile / smiled,* and so on. But some verbs, mostly verbs of very high frequency, have irregular past tenses: *see / saw, take / took, give / gave,* and so on. Children learning English acquire these frequent irregular forms early, and soon start saying *saw, took* and *gave*.

After a while, though, they begin learning the regular forms like *loved* and *washed*. Suddenly something clicks. The child realizes that there is a rule for making past tenses, and it delightedly starts saying *discovered*, *travelled* and *scraped*.

HOWEVER, AT THE SAME TIME, IT ABANDONS THE IRREGULAR FORMS LIKE **SAW** AND **TOOK**, AND IT BEGINS SAYING **SEED** AND **TAKED**.

... FORMS WHICH WE **NEVER** HEARD FROM ADULTS.

AFTER THAT, IT MUST ONCE AGAIN PAINFULLY LEARN THE IRREGULAR FORMS LIKE **SAW** AND **TOOK**.

Another observation is the acquisition of *negation*. At first, the child produces no negatives at all. Then it begins producing negative utterances by means of an invariable negative word – usually *no* in English – stuck at the beginning:

No I want milk.

Later, this *no* is moved next to the verb:

I no want milk.

Finally, the rather complicated English negative auxiliaries appear:

I don't want milk.

Example of Active Construction

A simple but striking example is the acquisition of English plurals. At first the child produces no plurals. Then, slowly, it learns enough regular plurals, such as *cats, biscuits* and *toys,* that it finally spots the rule, and begins happily producing new plurals with great freedom: *catalogues, lawnmowers, nurses.*

Small children can be tested to see if they have acquired this rule. A child is shown a cute little figure and told, *Look, here's a wug* – where *wug* is a made-up word it has never heard before. The tester continues, *Look, here's another wug. Now there are two...?* A child who correctly produces *wugs* has learned the rule.

If this is a WUG ...

... then what are these?

You yourself, of course, learned this rule long ago, and you apply it effortlessly every day to produce new plurals you have never encountered before: *CD-ROMs, laptops, e-mails, wusses.*

Such observations show clearly that the child cannot be proceeding by memorization or imitation. Instead, it must be constructing rules. And this is one of the most profound findings of modern linguistics: a child learning a first language *actively constructs* the language as it goes.

Indeed, most linguists are now satisfied that children are born with a biological language faculty, an innate disposition to acquire language. This innate faculty requires nothing more than a certain amount of stimulation from other people to be set in motion.

REMEMBER US DEAF NICARAGUAN CHILDREN.

WE CREATED A LANGUAGE FOR OURSELVES AS SOON AS WE WERE BROUGHT TOGETHER.

Creating a Language

We human beings can learn to do countless things. We can learn to do algebra, to make wine, to play the guitar, to dig oil wells, to prepare soufflés, to ice skate.

But these are only accomplishments. Billions of people go through their lives without ever learning these things. However, all healthy children, regardless of intelligence or circumstances, learn a first language, providing they have even the slightest opportunity to do so. As the Nicaraguan example shows, children are so determined to learn language that they will learn one even if they are not exposed to a language.

There are other cases that reinforce the same point.

Pidgin

Countless times in human history, people have been brought together in circumstances in which they had no language in common. This happened to Africans brought as slaves to the Americas. It happened to the workers brought from a dozen countries to work in the sugar plantations of Hawaii. And it has happened to the people of Papua New Guinea, recently united in a new nation with hundreds of indigenous languages.

In such circumstances, people invariably react in the same way...

.... WE CREATE A *PIDGIN*.

A pidgin is a crude and rudimentary language, with a small vocabulary and nothing much in the way of grammar. It is a poor and limited system of communication, but for simple purposes it does work, and everybody in the community learns to handle it.

Creoles

But then some people in the community get married and have children. And, whatever they may speak at home, the children have only the pidgin to speak with other children. The results are predictable.

IN ALMOST NO TIME, WE TAKE THIS PIDGIN AND TURN IT INTO A REAL LANGUAGE.

WE INTRODUCE ALL SORTS OF GRAMMATICAL ELABORATIONS, SUCH AS RELATIVE CLAUSES AND TENSE-MARKINGS, WHICH THE PIDGIN WE LEARNED DID NOT HAVE.

AND WE GREATLY EXPAND THE VOCABULARY SO THAT WE CAN SPEAK EASILY ABOUT ANYTHING WE LIKE.

In short, they create a new natural language, and the children who create it are the language's first native speakers. This new language is called a *creole*.

Just in the last few centuries, many dozens of creoles have appeared, in the Caribbean, in Africa, in Asia, in Hawaii, and elsewhere. All are testimony to that powerful human instinct to construct a language. When children construct a creole, not only do they learn a language their parents do not know, they learn a language that didn't even exist before – just like those deaf children in Nicaragua. Creoles, like Nicaraguan Sign Language, provide overpowering evidence that learning a first language is not merely an accomplishment, like learning to ice skate. Our language faculty is part of our **biology**, something that is built into our genes.

LIKE THE ECHO-LOCATION SYSTEM OF BATS ...

...OR THE LONG-DISTANCE NAVIGATIONAL SKILLS OF GEESE.

Our unique language faculty exists, most linguists now believe, because some of our remote ancestors evolved it. And, ever since that time, human children have been born with a biological urge to construct and use a language.

Chomsky's Universal Grammar

This "language urge" is unique to our species. As we saw earlier, no other creatures on the planet can even vaguely approach our ability to learn and use language. We can speak the way birds can sing, and for the same reasons. It is the recognition of our biological language faculty that has allowed linguists to join forces with psychologists, philosophers, computer scientists and students of artificial intelligence in laying the foundations of the new discipline called cognitive science. But just how much of our language is built into our genes?

The American linguist Noam Chomsky has for decades been arguing for a very strong view of our built-in linguistic endowment.

*I MAINTAIN THAT WE ARE BORN WITH A NUMBER OF HIGHLY SPECIFIC GRAMMATICAL RULES BUILT INTO OUR HEADS. THESE RULES I CALL **UNIVERSAL GRAMMAR** OR UG.*

Here is a possible example of UG. Consider the following English sentences, and ask yourself this question: in which sentences can the pronoun **she** possibly refer to Susie?

1. **Susie had a shower after she got up.**

2. **After she got up, Susie had a shower.**

3. **After Susie got up, she had a shower.**

4. **She had a shower after Susie got up.**

Could this be Susie?

All English speakers agree that **she** can possibly refer to **Susie** in the first three sentences, **but not in number four**.

But why? After all, all four sentences contain the same words, and all have very similar structures.

What is the Rule?

Well, there is a rule here. It has proved possible to formulate that rule with considerable precision, though only within the context of a carefully articulated theory of syntax. The first version, put forward by the American linguist Ronald Langacker in 1969, has a forbidding form:

An anaphor may not both precede and command its antecedent.

Current formulations of the rule differ somewhat, but are just as impenetrable to a reader who knows nothing of linguistic theory.

> NOW, ALL NATIVE SPEAKERS OF ENGLISH KNOW THIS RULE. WE NEVER VIOLATE IT WHEN SPEAKING, AND WE WOULD NEVER MISINTERPRET A SENTENCE LIKE (4) WHEN SOMEBODY ELSE USES IT.

But how did we learn this rule?

Our parents never taught us this rule. We didn't learn it in school. Indeed, most of us are not even aware that there is a rule here until somebody draws our attention to it.

Chomsky's proposed explanation is that this rule is part of UG. There is something in UG, something we are born with, which allows *she* to refer to *Susie* in three sentences but not in the fourth. In other words, this rule, like UG in general, is *innate*. We are just born with it.

YET, IN SOME POWERFUL SENSE, WE KNOW THE RULE ANYWAY. SOMEHOW, THE RULE HAS GOT INTO OUR HEADS. BUT HOW?

Linguistic Nativism

Chomsky's view that UG is innate is known as the hypothesis of *linguistic nativism*. And this hypothesis is deeply controversial. Many philosophers and psychologists – and also linguists – have reacted to it with anger or contempt. For many of these critics, nativism is not really a hypothesis, but only a retreat from scientific investigation.

*THE RULES ARE THERE BECAUSE THEY ARE THERE, AND HOW THEY GOT THERE IS NOT A **LINGUISTIC** ISSUE.*

Of course, we can try to evaluate the nativist claim here by investigating its supposedly universal nature. If Chomsky is right, then speakers of all human languages must have the same UG in their heads, and hence their languages must have more or less the same rules.

129

So, careful examination of the grammatical rules of a wide variety of languages should provide some evidence one way or the other. And, of course, some linguists have undertaken investigations of just this kind. But the task is not easy.

Most of the languages that are well known and that have been carefully investigated are European languages ...

But all these languages are related (they all descend from a single common ancestor). And, moreover, their speakers have been in intense contact for many centuries. Hence, all kinds of similarities among these languages are to be expected, for *non-biological* reasons.

Obstacles to Confirming UG

What we really need here is reliable and detailed information about a range of unrelated and geographically dispersed languages: say, some languages from the Americas, Africa, Siberia, southeast Asia, Australia and the Pacific.

BUT, FOR OBVIOUS PRACTICAL REASONS, VERY FEW OF THESE LANGUAGES HAVE SO FAR BEEN EXAMINED OR DESCRIBED IN GREAT DETAIL.

The linguists who are prepared to brave the unpleasantness of tropical rain forests, Siberian permafrost, local wars and other dangers are often linguists whose main interests and goals are not the kinds of theoretical issues that are relevant to the nativist hypothesis.

THEY JUST DON'T ASK THE RIGHT CRITICAL QUESTIONS.

These are formidable obstacles indeed. But we have, nevertheless, obtained a body of relevant data from a number of languages, data that we can scrutinize for possible confirmation or disconfirmation of nativist ideas. But the results, so far, have been largely of the most infuriating kind possible.

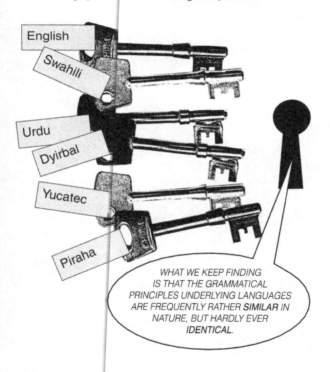

WHAT WE KEEP FINDING IS THAT THE GRAMMATICAL PRINCIPLES UNDERLYING LANGUAGES ARE FREQUENTLY RATHER **SIMILAR** IN NATURE, BUT HARDLY EVER **IDENTICAL**.

As a result, some followers of Chomsky's nativism have reacted by concluding that the principles of Universal Grammar must be more abstract than we had previously suspected. The principles can be stated only at a very high level of abstraction, remote from the surface forms of utterances, which result only from the interaction of the abstract principles with other devices and requirements.

Respectively, with Respect

But many critics have argued that this retreat into ever greater abstractness is futile and self-defeating: if we make our principles sufficiently abstract and sufficiently well insulated from the observable data, then these principles become unfalsifiable and untestable. That is, any given abstract principle can be made consistent with any set of data at all, and we no longer have a testable scientific hypothesis, but only an article of faith.

There are other problems. For example, certain important theoretical issues rest on the existence and interpretation of English *respectively* sentences, such as:

Jan and Larry drank whisky and sherry, respectively.

Some linguists have argued that the use of such sentences illustrates certain important things about UG. Unfortunately, other linguists have examined such sentences, and they have discovered something important and fascinating. Such sentences are used only by well-educated and highly literate speakers of English. In contrast, uneducated speakers of English not only do not use such sentences, they cannot even understand them when they are presented with them.

"RESPECTIVELY" DOESN'T MEAN WE DRANK SHERRY AND WHISKY "WITH RESPECT"...

BUT **HE** DRANK SHERRY AND **I** DRANK WHISKY.

Innate or Acquired?

So, it appears that *respectively* sentences cannot really tell us anything about our innate language faculty. Rather, the use and interpretation of such sentences appears to be something *acquired* only through formal education. But, if some of our linguistic behaviour is acquired only through education, and is not born with us, how can we be sure that any particular aspect of language use is innate rather than learned? And how, the critics ask, can we be sure that *any* aspect of language use is innate, as Chomsky claims ...

... OR MERELY LEARNED BY EXPERIENCE ...

– as suggested by the great Swiss psychologist Jean Piaget, among others?

Language Planning

Accordingly, while few linguists doubt that our language faculty is part of our biology, there are plenty of linguists who doubt that our language faculty is so detailed in its specifics as Chomsky suggests.

Anyway, we know that it is possible for the structure of a language to be substantially determined by political or educational programmes. In the 19th and 20th centuries, a number of European languages have come to be used for the first time as the national languages of new nation-states: Norwegian, Finnish, Bulgarian, Czech and others. In each case, it was necessary both to agree on a standard form for a language that had previously lacked one, and to create a huge body of new vocabulary for talking about technical subjects from philosophy to car engines, from linguistics to nuclear physics. This kind of work is called *language planning*, or *linguistic engineering*, and it is laborious and time-consuming.

Engineering Basque

Take the case of Basque, which has begun to be standardized only since the 1960s. Basque is spoken in the mountains of northern Spain and southwestern France. It had never before had a standard form, and it was spoken in numerous local varieties in the mountain valleys. Below is a small sample of the kind of local variation that faced the language planners when they began working on a new standard form.

"stone"	arri	harri		
"come"	etorri	ethorri	jin	jaugin
"word"	berba	itz	hitz	
"otter"	urtxakur	ugabere		
"I like it"	gustatzen jata	gustatzen zait	atsegin dut	laket zaut
"I'll do it"	eingo dot	egingo det	eginen dut	
"so long"	ikusi arte	ikhus arte		

Just imagine confronting thousands and thousands of regional differences like these, and trying to come up with a single set of agreed forms that will please everybody. But the Basques, after several decades, are now well advanced with their project, which should be completed in the foreseeable future – just as the Finns and others have already completed their own projects in language planning.

English has never undergone any language planning on this scale. This is not because English lacks regional or social variation – we have plenty – but only because our ancestors largely allowed a standard form of the language to emerge by a series of historical accidents, with no centralization and hardly any organized planning. This hit-or-miss approach has in fact been surprisingly successful at producing a single, rather unified standard form of English, with only minor regional differences.

AND IT IS THIS **STANDARD ENGLISH**, WITH ALL ITS WARTS AND ITS HISTORICAL CURIOSITIES, THAT WE LEARN IN SCHOOL AND USE FOR PUBLIC PURPOSES.

Standard English

Because of historical accidents, standard English requires:

I did it	and not	*I done it*
He doesn't know	and not	*He don't know*
I saw him	and not	*I seen him*
I haven't finished	and not	*I ain't finished*

and countless other forms that sound very odd indeed to uneducated speakers of vernacular English – not to mention that *respectively,* of course.

If somewhat different accidents had occurred, then ferocious English teachers would be doing their best to stamp out such "ignorant" and "illiterate" usages as *He doesn't do it* and *I saw it*, and teaching their pupils to use instead such refined and educated usages as *He don't do it* and *I seen it*.

I must allways write ain't.
I must allways write ain't.
I must allways write ain't.
I must allways write ain't.
I must allways write ain't.
I must allways write ain't.
I must allways write ain't
allways write ain
t, allways write ai
write ai

Sexism in Language

Language planning has not been prominent in English. But today some people are beginning to argue for some vigorous linguistic engineering of our language, and for a particular reason: sexism.

Like many languages, English has a good deal of sexism built into it.

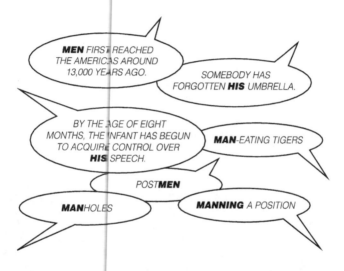

MEN FIRST REACHED THE AMERICAS AROUND 13,000 YEARS AGO.

SOMEBODY HAS FORGOTTEN HIS UMBRELLA.

BY THE AGE OF EIGHT MONTHS, THE INFANT HAS BEGUN TO ACQUIRE CONTROL OVER HIS SPEECH.

MAN-EATING TIGERS

POSTMEN

MANHOLES

MANNING A POSITION

We are now trying to find less sexist ways of speaking and writing. Sometimes simple solutions are available: *letter carrier* for *postman*, *chair* for *chairman*, *firefighter* for *fireman*. Other cases are more awkward.

Somebody has forgotten his or her umbrella?

Somebody has forgotten their umbrella?

There appears to be no way out that will please everybody.

Sexist Attitudes

Even if we could somehow legislate these undesirable usages into oblivion, doing so wouldn't get rid of sexist attitudes. We constantly read things like these: *He attacked his next-door neighbour's wife* (the woman wasn't his neighbour?); *The pioneers trekked across the prairies with their cattle, their seed corn, and their wives* (the wives were just there as what?).

The new editor of The New Yorker is a striking and willowy blonde.

(Would a male editor be described like this?)

Unappealing as such usages are, most linguists consider their primary job to be recording and describing the language as it is, and not to be trying to change it. That is, the attitude of linguists is *descriptivism*, as opposed to the prescriptivism discussed earlier in the book. This fact has often led to misunderstanding among the wider public of what linguists are trying to do.

Descriptivism

Non-linguists often accuse linguists of maintaining that "any sort of language is equally good", particularly when we decline to join them in their passionate campaigns against whatever it is that has irked them. But this is misguided. Individual linguists have their own ideas about what constitutes good or appropriate usage in English, just like anybody else – except that the linguists' views are usually far better informed than other people's. But there is a big difference between expressing opinions and finding out what the facts are, and it is finding the facts that is the primary task of a linguist. Nobody would attack a botanist merely because that botanist was interested in finding out what plants are like,

instead of creating beautiful gardens.

Disordered Language

All the examples we have considered so far represent normal language use. But not all language use is normal. Most particularly, our language can become abnormal, or *disordered*, when we are suffering from an injury to the brain. This happens because certain areas of the brain are largely dedicated to the use of language, and damage to these areas therefore disrupts our language.

Disordered language resulting from brain damage is called *aphasia* (or *dysphasia*), and several different types are known.

In the 1860s, the French surgeon Paul Broca identified a particular disorder now called *Broca's aphasia*. A sufferer from this aphasia speaks painfully slowly and laboriously, with very little in the way of grammar, and his speech is somewhat slurred.

THE SUFFERER'S COMPREHENSION IS LARGELY INTACT, AND HIS SPEECH MAKES SENSE, EVEN THOUGH IT MAY BE HARD FOR OTHERS TO WORK OUT.

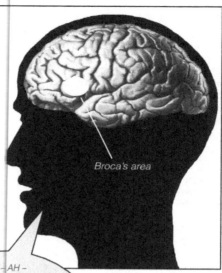

Post-mortem investigation of eight such patients showed that all had suffered injury to a particular area on the left side of the brain, now called *Broca's area*. Broca conjectured that this area must therefore be responsible for providing the grammatical structure of sentences, and also for the fine muscular control of the speech organs. These conclusions are now known to be correct.

Wernicke's Aphasia

In the 1870s, the Austrian neurologist Carl Wernicke identified a group of patients with a very different form of aphasia, now called *Wernicke's aphasia*. A sufferer speaks rapidly and fluently, with normal rhythm and intonation, but what he says makes no sense.

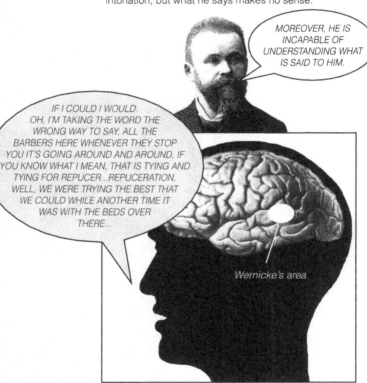

MOREOVER, HE IS INCAPABLE OF UNDERSTANDING WHAT IS SAID TO HIM.

IF I COULD I WOULD. OH, I'M TAKING THE WORD THE WRONG WAY TO SAY, ALL THE BARBERS HERE WHENEVER THEY STOP YOU IT'S GOING AROUND AND AROUND, IF YOU KNOW WHAT I MEAN, THAT IS TYING AND TYING FOR REPUCER...REPUCERATION, WELL, WE WERE TRYING THE BEST THAT WE COULD WHILE ANOTHER TIME IT WAS WITH THE BEDS OVER THERE...

Wernicke's area

Post-mortem investigations again revealed that all the patients had suffered injury to another part of the left side of the brain, now called *Wernicke's area*. Wernicke's area appears to be responsible both for comprehension and for access to ordinary vocabulary.

Neurolinguistics

Since Broca's and Wernicke's days, *neurolinguistics,* as we now call the study of language functioning within the brain, has made considerable advances. Today we no longer have to wait for post-mortems on the brains of deceased sufferers: we can study the linguistic behaviour of the brains of living, healthy, conscious people by using brain scanners to detect activity. These studies have broadly confirmed the earlier results, but, at the same time, complex new problems have arisen.

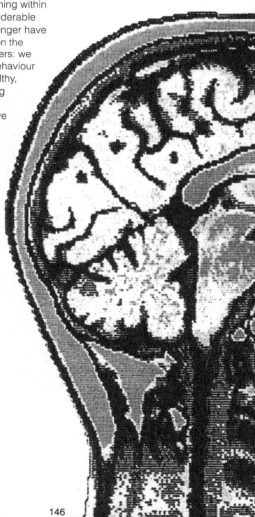

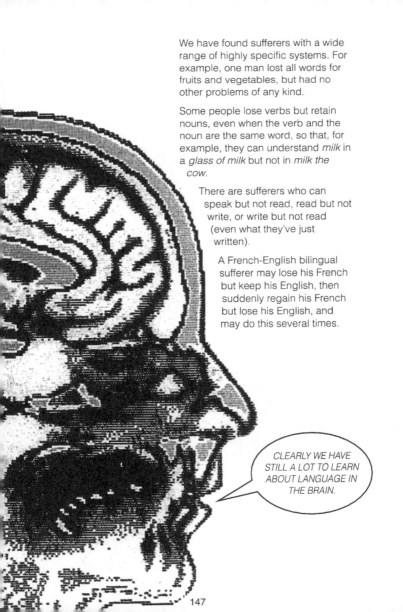

We have found sufferers with a wide range of highly specific systems. For example, one man lost all words for fruits and vegetables, but had no other problems of any kind.

Some people lose verbs but retain nouns, even when the verb and the noun are the same word, so that, for example, they can understand *milk* in a *glass of milk* but not in *milk the cow*.

There are sufferers who can speak but not read, read but not write, or write but not read (even what they've just written).

A French-English bilingual sufferer may lose his French but keep his English, then suddenly regain his French but lose his English, and may do this several times.

CLEARLY WE HAVE STILL A LOT TO LEARN ABOUT LANGUAGE IN THE BRAIN.

Specific Language Impairment

Not all linguistic deficits result from brain damage. Some of them appear to be caused by genetic abnormalities. A good example is the curious disability called *Specific Language Impairment*, or SLI. Sufferers from SLI are fairly normal in most respects, but they have a terrible time with grammatical words and endings. They can't learn them or produce them accurately, and often leave them out altogether, or occasionally put them in where they don't belong ...

Yesterday I eat two cookie.

There be a trains coming.

Most spectacularly, they fail the *wug* test described above: asked to form the plural of a nonsense word, they have no idea what it might be. For *wug*, they produce ...

– or something equally surprising; for *zat* they produce *zacko;* for *zash* they produce *zatches;* and so on.

It appears that sufferers from SLI have never learned that there are rules for making things like plurals. Consequently, they must painfully learn all the regular plurals like *dogs* and *boxes* one by one, just as we all do with the irregular ones like *men* and *mice*. As a result, they have no idea what the plural of a new noun might be, since they have no rule to fall back on.

Williams Syndrome

Another linguistic disability which results from a faulty gene is the *Williams syndrome*. Sufferers from this syndrome exhibit a number of physical abnormalities, including unusual pixie-like faces, as well as a severe degree of mental retardation, so severe that they cannot look after themselves and must live in institutions. Williams sufferers have absolutely no trouble in learning linguistic rules: for example, they learn to construct regular plurals like *books* and regular past tenses like *enjoyed* as readily as anyone else. But they do have a linguistic problem of another kind.

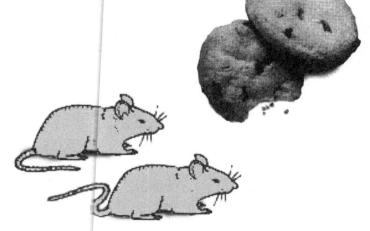

They have some difficulty in finding words. It is not that they hesitate or stumble – in fact, they typically speak in a breathless rush – but that they often select the wrong words. So, for example, a Williams sufferer may say *parrot* when *sparrow* is intended, or *cake* when *cookie* is meant. Moreover, they not infrequently overgeneralize the rules they know so well, and, like very young children, say *taked* instead of *took* or *mouses* instead of *mice*.

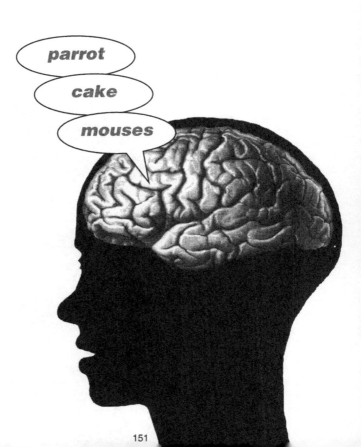

A Psycholinguistic View of Language

In his recent book *Words and Rules*, the Canadian psycholinguist Steven Pinker assembles evidence from first-language acquisition, from normal adult behaviour, and from SLI and Williams sufferers, to develop a general view of how language operates in the mind. Pinker argues that our language faculty consists of two large, important and distinct components.

One component is the **storage**, or **look-up**, element.

> IN THIS, LINGUISTIC ITEMS ARE LEARNED ONE AT A TIME, MEMORIZED, STORED AWAY ON FILE, AND THEN LOOKED UP WHENEVER THEY ARE NEEDED.

We all need to do this when we learn words or things. English speakers must learn that a certain large snouted animal is called a *pig*, Welsh speakers learn that the animal is called a *mochyn*, speakers of German a *Schwein*, of Basque a *txerri*, of Yimas (in New Guinea) a *numbran*, and so on.

Likewise, we must simply learn, store and look up the irregular forms like *mice* and *took*.

The other component is the **rules** which we gradually construct during acquisition, rules (in English) like "Make a plural by adding -*s*" and "Make a past tense by adding -*ed*".

Both components are essential: the rules are useless if we haven't memorized some things to apply them to, while doing without rules would mean we would have to memorize and look up absolutely everything – a formidable task.

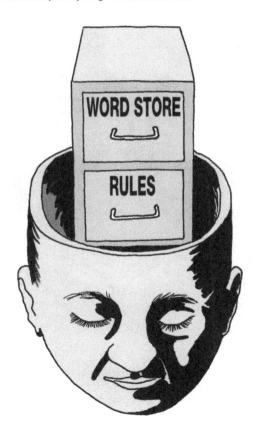

A Problem of Faulty Genes

Pinker (and others) argue that SLI disability is largely a deficit in the rule component.

WILLIAMS SYNDROME SUFFERERS LEARN THE RULES ALL RIGHT, BUT THEIR STORAGE AND LOOK-UP FACILITY IS ERRATIC AND OFTEN FAILS TO RETRIEVE THE REQUIRED ITEM.

SLI SUFFERERS NEVER LEARN THE RULES AND MUST PROCEED BY TRYING TO MEMORIZE JUST ABOUT EVERYTHING, WITH COMPLICATED CONSEQUENCES.

Geneticists have recently pinpointed the locations of both of the faulty genes implicated in producing SLI and the Williams syndrome. Perhaps, one day, we will be able to identify precisely what is going wrong in the brain when these genes are defective, and thus to understand something about the way the brain processes language.

How Did Language Originate?

Related to our hope of understanding language in the brain is another hope: the hope of learning something about how language came into existence in the first place. For many years, this very topic was taboo among linguists. That's because nothing of significance was known about the structure of language, about the functioning of the brain or about language processing in the brain, or even about human ancestry. Indeed, in 1867 the French Academy of Sciences banned discussion of the topic.

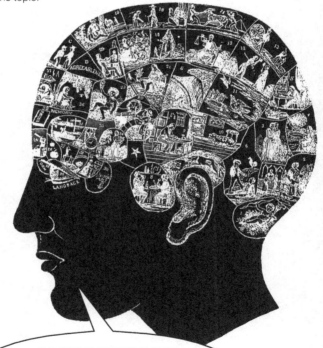

AND WITH GOOD REASON, SINCE NOTHING WAS BEING OFFERED BUT SPECULATIONS AND FANTASIES, OFTEN VERY ABSURD ONES.

What Do We Know Today?

Today we are much better off. Linguists can tell us important things about the way languages are put together. Psycholinguists have made great progress in understanding how language is processed in the mind. Neurolinguists and neurologists now know a great deal about the way the brain is structured, how it behaves, and how language is located and organized in the brain. And, of course, palaeoanthropologists have made huge progress in unravelling the origins of our species. So we now have a body of facts to work with.

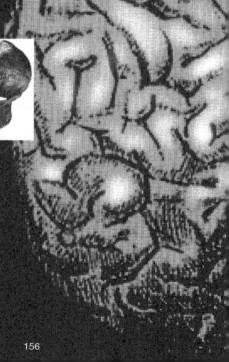

156

But that doesn't mean we are much closer to answering the question of *how, when* or *why* language began. Linguists are now beginning to hold regular discussions with specialists in many other fields – *psychologists, anthropologists, primatologists* (specialists in primates, the group that includes apes and monkeys as well as human beings), *archaeologists*, and other interested scientists, in the hope of finding some common ground. However, little has yet been found.

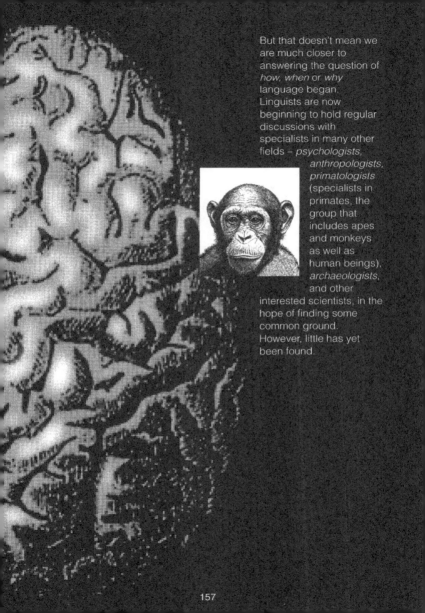

When Did Language Begin?

How early did language arise? Some archaeologists and anthropologists believe they can see evidence for a long period of virtual stasis in the culture of our ancestors...

... FOLLOWED BY A SUDDEN AND BRILLIANT BLOSSOMING OF ART, TECHNOLOGY AND CULTURE AROUND 40–50,000 YEARS AGO.

This date must represent the first appearance of language, since nothing else could explain this explosive development. Others, including most linguists, conclude that our language faculty is so much a part of our biology that language must have appeared together with our own species, *Homo sapiens*, between 100,000 and 200,000 years ago.

Then again, some anthropologists are convinced that the fossil skulls of our hominid ancestors who lived over a million years ago, before our own species had evolved, show clear evidence of the brain structures associated with language, such as Broca's area.

*THEY CONCLUDE THAT LANGUAGE MUST BE EVEN OLDER THAN **HOMO SAPIENS**.*

There is no consensus, since the new data available to us point in different directions.

The Gradualist Theory

Did language emerge gradually or suddenly? We don't know. On the one hand, the psycholinguist Stephen Pinker and his colleague Paul Bloom have argued that language must have emerged slowly and gradually, in tiny increments, in response to the pressures of natural selection. In this view, early hominids who were slightly better at using language had an adaptive advantage over their less eloquent kinfolk. So they survived better and produced more offspring, with the result that linguistically skilful individuals gradually took over the world, by out-competing their more tongue-tied neighbours.

UG

UGH UGH

FOOD

WE HUNT

MANY BUFFALO THERE

DON'T ATTACK UNTIL I SAY

LET'S TAKE THE KILL BACK TO THE OTHERS

I HAVE SEEN HERDS OF ANTELOPE OVER THE HILL. I THINK WE SHOULD MOVE THERE.

LET'S SPEND THE WINTER HERE. IT'S MORE SHELTERED AND THERE ARE ANIMALS TO HUNT.

BECAUSE OUR LANGUAGE SKILLS GOT BETTER, WE SURVIVED BETTER. BUT IT ALL HAPPENED SLOWLY AND GRADUALLY.

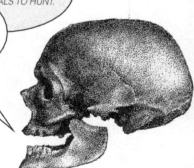

The Catastrophic Theory

On the other hand, the British-born American linguist Derek Bickerton has argued for a sudden, indeed catastrophic, emergence of language. In Bickerton's view, our ancestors had no language for a long time, but they gradually acquired brain structures that permitted ever more sophisticated mental operations.

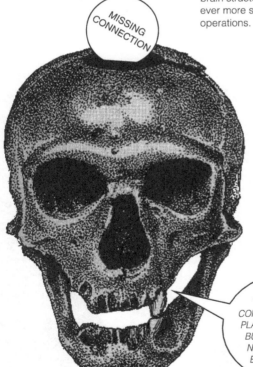

Criticism of the Gradualist View

The Pinker–Bloom view suffers from a difficulty in imagining what a partial language might look like. Can we envision a "language" with nouns but no verbs, or with affirmative statements but no negative statements, or with sentences of two words but not of ten words, or with names for things but practically no grammar? Linguists find this hard to accept. No such "language" has ever been found anywhere – except for the last.

This last describes the pidgin languages, which have tiny vocabularies and practically no grammar. As we have seen, pidgins are created by people who need to communicate but who have no language in common.

Bickerton's point is that nothing ever seems to be observed that lies somewhere between pidgins and real languages. He notes several other related features to pidgin. Systems strikingly similar to pidgins can be observed among very young children just starting to acquire their mother tongues.

Also among certain individuals suffering from brain damage. And even among chimpanzees to which scientists have tried hard to teach some form of human language.

Bickerton's Conclusion

Bickerton concludes, therefore, that there exist only two linguistic possibilities, a crude pidgin-like system which he calls protolanguage, and full-blown human language. Our remote ancestors must therefore have jumped pretty much overnight from the one to the other, thanks to the sudden acquisition of some crucial connection in the brain.

For Bickerton, children acquire protolanguage before they move on to language, certain damaged individuals never acquire anything beyond protolanguage, and our relatives the great apes, having never acquired that last fateful connection in their brains, can be taught to manage protolanguage but not language.

Another Cognitive Example

Nothing is settled. Nor do we as yet even have any great agreement as to whether language should be regarded as an entirely distinct phenomenon, or whether it should be viewed as an integral part of our perception and cognition. Recall the ideas of the cognitive linguists, discussed above, in which linguistic categories are seen as *perceptual* and *metaphorical* categories. And now consider one further example of the cognitive approach.

In English, if we say that

a cockerel is *at the back of the house*

– where is the bird?

> OF COURSE, IT'S BEHIND THE HOUSE, AT THE SIDE OPPOSITE THE FRONT.

Fine. But, in quite a number of languages, above all in parts of Africa, when speakers describe a bird as (literally) "at the back of the house"...

> WE MEAN THAT IT IS ON THE ROOF.

How do we understand this difference?

Differences of Metaphor

Well, in English, it appears, we orient ourselves in terms of *human beings*. And our backs are behind us. So, something which is "at our back" is behind us. But not all languages work in the same way – that is, they don't all use the *same metaphors*. The speakers of some languages think metaphorically, not in terms of people, but in terms of four-footed animals, such as buffalo.

*AND WHERE IS A BIRD WHICH IS "ON THE BACK" OF A BUFFALO? THAT'S RIGHT: ON **TOP** OF IT.*

So, a different choice of metaphor produces different senses for the same words. And the cognitive linguists are arguing that almost nothing can be expressed in any human language without the selection of a metaphor through which to express it.

Indeed, there are linguists, such as Robins Burling, who argue that seeing language as primarily a means of communication is an error. Language, proposes Burling, is best seen as a means of organizing the world, as a way of constructing and organizing mental representations. In this view, our familiar ability to communicate with language is merely a spin-off – though admittedly a very valuable spin-off – of our linguistic cognition.

But it remains true that we know next to nothing about the way in which language came into existence. Naturally, into this void have come countless speculations, not a few of them confident in tone and even strident.

Conflicting Speculations

Some people argue that our remote
ancestors must have gestured before
they could speak, and that speech
must have grown out of gestures.

OTHERS ARGUE THAT
LANGUAGE AROSE SPECIFICALLY
BECAUSE IT WAS VALUABLE IN
CONSTRUCTING AND USING
TOOLS ...

... OR BECAUSE SPEAKING
WAS A WONDERFULLY EFFECTIVE WAY
OF ATTRACTING MATES ...

... OR BECAUSE WE WERE
EAGER TO GOSSIP ...

This last view sees speech as a kind of vocal grooming, replacing the constant grooming behaviour seen in apes today.

The Purposes of Language

The best that can be said about these competing interpretations is that all of them are highly implausible. It is most unlikely that language arose in order to serve any *one* particular purpose, and that only later did our ancestors discover that it could also be pressed into service for *other* purposes. In fact, we use language for a wide range of purposes. Here are just a few:

- **passing on information**
- **persuading people to do things**
- **convincing people to believe things**
- **entertaining others**
- **amusing ourselves**
- **maintaining and displaying our place in society**
- **expressing our individuality**
- **expressing our emotion**
- **maintaining good (or bad) relations with others**

Few linguists are eager to believe that our ancestors evolved language purely in order to serve just one of these numerous functions, and then accidentally discovered that they could use it for one or two other things as well. Language is richer than that, and it is more deeply embedded in our existence. Language, remember, is what most obviously distinguishes us from all the other creatures that live on this planet.

MORE THAN ANYTHING ELSE, LANGUAGE IS WHAT MAKES US HUMAN.

*AND, IN SPITE OF OUR OBVIOUS AND IMPRESSIVE PROGRESS IN UNDERSTANDING ITS NATURE, WE STILL HAVE A LONG WAY TO GO BEFORE WE CAN SAY THAT WE KNOW **WHAT** LANGUAGE IS.*

Further Reading

If you'd like to learn more about linguistics, this chatty and very readable book is a good place to start:

R.L. Trask. 1999. *Language: The Basics*, 2nd edition. London: Routledge.

Beyond this, you can move on to a textbook. Here is an elementary text:

Jean Aitchison. 1992. *Teach Yourself Linguistics*, 4th edition. London: Hodder.

Larger, but still elementary, is this:

George Yule. 1996. *The Study of Language*, 2nd edition. Cambridge: Cambridge University Press.

Larger still, but brightly written, is this one:

Victoria Fromkin and Robert Rodman. 1998. *An Introduction to Language*, 6th edition. Fort Worth: Harcourt Brace.

The first reference book to consult is this gloriously illustrated encyclopedia:

David Crystal. 1997. *The Cambridge Encyclopedia of Language*, 2nd edition. Cambridge: Cambridge University Press.

If you're interested in the history of linguistics, there are lots of books, but not all of them are easy to read. For the period before the 20th century, try this:

R.H. Robins. 1967. *A Short History of Linguistics*. London: Longman.

The 20th century is more difficult, but try this one, which is a little selective:

Geoffrey Sampson. 1980. *Schools of Linguistics*. London: Hutchinson

For a collection of enjoyable popular essays on recent hot topics, look for this:

Jay Ingram. 1992. *Talk Talk Talk*. London: Penguin.

For psycholinguistics and child language acquisition, this is the most readable textbook:

Jean Aitchison. 1998. *The Articulate Mammal*, 4th edition. London: Routledge.

The next book introduces language and brain:

Loraine K. Obler and Kris Gjerlow. 1999. *Language and the Brain*. Cambridge: Cambridge University Press.

There are two lively introductions to anthropological linguistics:

Nancy Bonvillain. 1993. *Language, Culture, and Communication*. Englewood Cliffs: Prentice Hall.

Gary B. Palmer. 1996. *Toward a Theory of Cultural Linguistics*. Austin: University of Texas Press.

An elementary book on language change is this:

R.L. Trask. 1994. *Language and Change*. London: Routledge.

Finally, a splendid coffee table book on the languages of the world:

Bernard Comrie et al. 1997. *The Atlas of Languages*. London: Bloomsbury.

Index

Biographies

R.L. Trask is professor of Linguistics at the University of Sussex. A specialist in historical linguistics and in the Basque language, he is the author of numerous books, including *Language: The Basics, Language Change, Historical Linguistics, The History of Basque* and *A Student's Dictionary of Language and Linguistics*.

Bill Mayblin trained as a graphic designer at the Royal College of Art in London. He is a senior partner in the London-based design practice, Information Design Workshop.